Rhone `

Guide 2024

Explore History, Culture,

and Beauty

Bernard E. Williams

Table of Contents

Map of Rhone

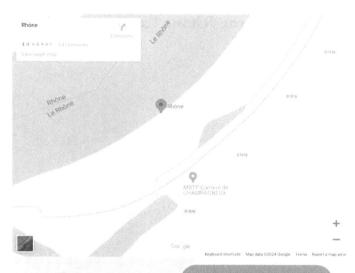

How To Use

1. Open QR code reader app
2. Scan the QR code with camera
3. View the contents

INTRODUCTION

Overview of the Rhone Region

The Rhone region in southeastern France is a diversified area recognized for its beautiful scenery, rich history, and vibrant culture. The region is called for the Rhone River, which runs through it, providing scenic views and fertile land for grapes. Lyon, France's third-largest city, is famed for its historical and architectural treasures; Vienne, noted for its Roman remains and jazz festival; and Valence, which serves as a gateway to the magnificent Vercors mountains.

The region's natural features, including the Rhône River Valley, Mont Pilat, and the Ardèche Gorges, make it a haven for nature lovers and outdoor enthusiasts.

Historical Significance: The Rhone region has made major contributions to both French and European heritage. The region played an important role in the Roman Empire, as evidenced by the well-preserved Roman theaters at Lyon and Vienne. Lyon, a UNESCO World Heritage Site, was formerly the Gauls' capital before becoming a major silk trade city during the Renaissance. The Basilica of Notre-Dame de Fourvière and Lyon's ancient Old Town are notable architectural landmarks.

The Rhone area also played an important role in the French Resistance during World War II, particularly in cities such as Lyon, which were famed for their underground networks.

Main Attractions and Activities: The Rhone region offers a variety of attractions and activities. Key attractions include Lyon's Basilica of Notre-Dame de Fourvière, the Hauterives' Palais Idéal du Facteur Cheval, and the Côtes du Rhône wineries. Outdoor opportunities abound, including hiking paths in the Monts du Lyonnais, cycling along the Via Rhôna, and kayaking in the Ardèche Gorges. Cultural events include visiting Lyon's Museum of Fine Arts, attending the Fête des Lumières festival, and shopping at local markets. Culinary delights are highlighted, with the opportunity to relish traditional dishes, participate in wine excursions, and sample regional specialties.

Purpose of the Guide

This travel guide aims to provide tourists with thorough, practical, and up-to-date information on the Rhone region. Readers may anticipate deep insights into the area's history, culture, attractions, and activities, allowing them to plan and enjoy a wonderful trip. The guide strives to meet the demands of real-time travelers by providing suggestions, recommendations, and local insights to enhance their experience.

History and Culture

The Rhone region has a rich and diverse history, stretching from ancient times to the present. Cities such as Lyon (Lugdunum) and Vienne thrived as commercial and cultural hubs throughout the Roman era. The medieval period saw the creation of magnificent cathedrals and fortifications, reflecting the region's strategic importance. Throughout the Renaissance, Lyon became a silk trade and banking center, which helped the city's economic and cultural development. The nineteenth and twentieth centuries saw industrialization and major urban expansion, which shaped the contemporary Rhone region.

The Rhone region has rich traditions, customs, and festivals. Annual celebrations of the region's rich cultural heritage include the Fête des Lumières in Lyon, the Jazz à Vienne festival, and grape harvest festivals. Unique cultural practices, such as traditional silk weaving in Lyon and winemaking in the Côtes du Rhône, provide travelers with insight into the region's artisanal traditions. The Rhone region's culinary tradition, which includes dishes such as French coq au vin and quenelles, reflects agricultural abundance and gastronomic inventiveness.

The Rhone region's cultural landmarks include the Museum of Fine Arts of Lyon, which houses a diverse collection of art from antiquity to present times. The Roman theaters at Lyon and Vienne are outstanding examples of ancient architecture, and they continue to hold performances today. Lyon's ancient Old Town, with its narrow cobblestone alleyways and

Renaissance architecture, provides a beautiful look back in time. Art galleries, historical buildings, and municipal museums throughout the region offer visitors diverse cultural experiences.

The Rhone region's history and culture greatly impact its current lifestyle and attractions. Modern cultural events, such as the Biennale de la Danse in Lyon and several music festivals, are inspired by the region's artistic legacy. The culinary landscape, which includes modern chefs and traditional markets, demonstrates a strong appreciation for local foods and culinary traditions. Lifestyle trends, such as a focus on sustainable living and unhurried travel, are consistent with the region's long standing emphasis on workmanship and quality.

The Rhone area has had several remarkable figures who have helped shape its history and culture. These include the Roman Emperor Claudius, born in Lyon; the 19th-century chef

Marie-Antoine Carême, who revolutionized French cuisine; and the Lumière brothers, movie pioneers. Contemporary influencers, including chefs Paul Bocuse and Anne-Sophie Pic, continue to impact the region's cultural landscape by promoting its culinary quality and innovative attitude.

As you go through this guide, you will find images of notable landmarks and destinations, each accompanied by a QR code. Scan the QR code on the image to access a map and get directions to that location. Let's start exploring!

Chapter One

Planning Your Trip

The best time to visit

Seasonal Highlights

Spring (March-May): The Rhone area offers pleasant temperatures and flowering scenery, perfect for outdoor activities like hiking and cycling. Vineyards begin to come alive, making it an ideal time for wine tasting.

Summer (June-August): Summer is warm and bright, making it ideal for experiencing the region's cities and outdoor activities. It is also festival season, with several activities taking place. However, it can become busy, particularly in major tourist destinations.

Autumn (September-November): This is the harvest season; therefore, it is a wonderful time for wine lovers to visit. The weather stays mild, and the fall foliage enhances the panoramic magnificence.

Winter (December-February): The Rhone area has moderate winters, making it ideal for touring cities without the summer crowds. It's also an excellent time to sample robust local cuisine and visit indoor cultural attractions.

Festivals and Events

Fête des Lumières (December): Lyon has a stunning light festival with artistic displays that dazzle the city.

Jazz à Vienne (June-July) is a well-known jazz festival held in Vienne, featuring performances by international jazz artists.

Vinum (April): A wine festival in the Côtes du Rhône featuring tastings and vineyard tours.

Les Nuits de Fourvière (June-August): Lyon's arts festival with music, theater, and dance events.

Crowd Levels and Tourism Trends

Peak Season (June-August): High visitor influx, particularly in towns like Lyon and popular sites. It is recommended that you make reservations in advance.

Shoulder Seasons (Spring and Autumn): Moderate crowds, making it ideal for a more leisurely experience with excellent weather.

Off-Peak Season (Winter): Fewer tourists, resulting in a quieter experience and easier access to major attractions.

Special considerations

Weather Conditions: Pack according to the season, including layers for spring and autumn and sunscreen for summer.

Public Holiday: Be careful of French public holidays, as some attractions may be closed and transportation may be restricted.

Local customs: Familiarize yourself with

French etiquette, such as handshakes or cheek kisses, as well as proper dining manners.

Insider Tip: Visit popular wineries early in the morning or late in the day to avoid crowds.

Visit big sights on weekdays to avoid crowds.

Take advantage of local markets and festivals to gain unique cultural experiences.

How to Get There

1. Air Travel

Main Airports: Lyon-Saint-Exupéry Airport (LYS) is the main international airport, with flights from major cities worldwide. Call +33 826 80 08 26 to book a flight.

Airlines: Major airlines, such as Air France, Lufthansa, and British Airways, provide frequent service.

Connections: Direct flights from Paris, London, Frankfurt, and New York. Regional airports such as Grenoble and Saint-Étienne provide domestic and limited international flights.

2. Train Travel

High-Speed Trains (TGV): The TGV connects Lyon to Paris in around 2 hours, as well as other significant cities such as Marseille and Geneva.

Regional Trains: TER trains connect smaller villages and cities across the Rhone area.

International Connections: Eurostar and other international trains connect the Rhone region to adjacent nations.

3. Bus and Coach Services

Major Operators: FlixBus and Ouibus provide service in Lyon and surrounding cities.

Numerous routes connect major French cities to neighboring countries.

Advantages: Reasonably priced and comfy, with gorgeous views.

4. Driving and Car Rentals

Major Highways: The A7 (Autoroute du Soleil) connects Lyon and Marseille in the Rhone region.

Scenic Routes: Routes through vineyards and farmland provide stunning vistas.

Car Rental: Available in major airports and cities. A valid driver's license and a credit card are required. Learn about French driving regulations.

5. Alternative transportation

River Cruises: Enjoy a leisurely exploration of the Rhone River region.

The Via Rhôna cycling route runs along the Rhone River from Lake Geneva to the Mediterranean, offering a gorgeous and energetic way to travel.

Organized excursions: Several tour operators provide guided excursions based on specialized interests such as wine, history, and outdoor activities.

Travel Documents and Visa Requirements

1. Passport Requirements: Travelers must have a passport that is valid for at least three months beyond their anticipated departure date from the Schengen Area. Ensure that the passport contains blank pages for entry and departure stamps.

2. Visa Requirements

Visa-Free Travel: Citizens of the EU, EEA, and numerous other countries (including the USA, Canada, and Australia) do not require a visa for visits of up to 90 days during a 180-day period.

Schengen Visa: Required for visitors from countries that are not on the visa-free list. In your own country, apply to the French consulate or embassy.

The Application Process: Submit an application form, passport images, proof of trip insurance, lodging, and financial resources.

3. Customs and Immigration

Declare significant sums of cash, expensive goods, and specific food products. Before you travel, check the duty-free allowances and limits.

Upon arrival, produce your passport, visa (if applicable), and any other necessary papers. Prepare to answer questions regarding your stay.

4. Travel Insurance is highly recommended for all travelers.

Insurance should cover medical emergencies, vacation cancellations, lost luggage, and personal liabilities.

Consider policies that cover certain activities, like adventure sports or wine trips.

5. Local Laws and Regulations

Photography: Respect privacy and do not photograph individuals without permission. Some places may have photographic limitations.

Public Behavior: Be respectful and polite.

Public intoxication and disorderly behavior are discouraged.

Cultural Practices: Respect local norms, such as greeting manners and dress restrictions, especially at religious sites.

Language and Useful Phrases

Official Language: French is the official language of the Rhone region. It is widely used in everyday life, including in signs, menus, and public transportation. While many locals may speak some English, especially in tourist areas, knowing basic French can enhance your travel experience.

Commonly Spoken Languages: In addition to French, English is commonly spoken in tourist areas, hotels, and restaurants. You might also encounter regional dialects and accents, especially in rural areas.

Basic French Phrases

Greetings:

- Bonjour (bohn-zhoor) - Hello
- Bonsoir (bohn-swahr) - Good evening
- Salut (sa-loo) - Hi/Bye (informal)

Polite Expressions:

- Merci (mehr-see) - Thank you
- S'il vous plaît (seel voo pleh) - Please
- Excusez-moi (ehk-skew-zay mwah) - Excuse me

Common Questions:

- Où est...? (oo eh) - Where is...?
- Combien ça coûte? (kohm-byen sah koot) - How much does it cost?
- Parlez-vous anglais? (par-lay voo ahn-glay) - Do you speak English?

Travel-Specific Phrases

Directions:

- Pouvez-vous m'aider? (poo-vay voo meh-day) - Can you help me?

- Où se trouve...? (oo suh troov) - Where is...?

Ordering Food:

- Je voudrais... (zhuh voo-dray) - I would like...

- L'addition, s'il vous plaît (lah-dee-syon, seel voo pleh) - The bill, please

Hotel Check-In:

- J'ai une réservation (zhay oon ray-zair-vah-syon) - I have a reservation

- À quelle heure est le check-out? (ah kehl uhr eh luh check-out) - What time is check-out?

Pronunciation Tips

French pronunciation can be tricky. Practice common sounds, such as the nasal "n" and the guttural "r."

Phonetic Spellings:

- Merci (mehr-see)
- Bonjour (bohn-zhoor)

Listen to audio examples or use language apps to hear and practice correct pronunciation.

Cultural Etiquette

Address people formally using "Monsieur" (Mr.) or "Madame" (Mrs./Ms.).

Use polite expressions like "s'il vous plaît" and "merci" frequently.

It's customary to greet shopkeepers and say goodbye when leaving.

Language Apps and Resources

Duolingo: A popular app for learning basic French.

Google Translate: Helpful for translating phrases on the go.

YouTube Channels: Many offer free French language lessons and pronunciation guides.

Emergency Phrases:

- À l'aide! (ah lehd) - Help!
- Appelez la police! (ah-peh-lay lah poh-lees) - Call the police!

Medical Assistance:

- J'ai besoin d'un médecin (zhay buh-zwan dun may-deh-sahn) - I need a doctor
- Où est l'hôpital le plus proche? (oo eh loh-pee-tal luh ploo prohsh) - Where is the nearest hospital?

Health and Safety Tips

1. Healthcare Facilities: The Rhone region has excellent healthcare facilities, such as hospitals, clinics, and pharmacies. Major cities like Lyon have well-equipped hospitals, such as the Hospices Civils de Lyon. Pharmacies are widespread and easily identifiable by their

green crosses. Emergency medical services are readily available, and ambulances run throughout the region.

2. Travel Health Insurance: Those visiting the Rhone region should strongly consider purchasing travel health insurance. Ensure that your coverage covers medical emergencies, hospital stays, and repatriation. Some insurance also covers trip cancellations, lost luggage, and other travel-related incidents.

3. Vaccination and Health Precautions: For travel to the Rhone area, there are no required immunizations. However, standard vaccinations such as measles, mumps, rubella (MMR), and diphtheria-tetanus-pertussis should be kept up-to-date. If you plan to stay for an extended period of time or visit rural areas, consider getting hepatitis A and B vaccinations.

4. Safety Tip: Be mindful of your surroundings and safeguard personal belongings. Avoid showing valuable stuff publicly. Be cautious in

crowded areas where pickups may occur. Avoid dark, secluded regions at night. Familiarize yourself with local scams and how to avoid them, such as fraudulent petitions or too pleasant acquaintances.

5. Important Emergency Numbers

Police: 17, ambulances: 15, and firefighters: 18. The European emergency number is 112.

Keep the contact information for your country's consulate or embassy ready.

6. Natural Hazards: The Rhone region is prone to floods, particularly following heavy rainfall. Keep up with weather forecasts and local alerts.

When trekking or partaking in outdoor sports, exercise caution because the terrain might be harsh and weather conditions can change quickly.

7. Local Laws and Regulations: To ensure your safety and compliance, be aware of local rules and regulations. Public intoxication and disruptive behavior are not acceptable.

Photographing some government buildings and military facilities is illegal. Respect local customs and cultural practices, particularly at holy sites.

Budget and Costs

1. Typical Travel Costs: The Rhone area offers a variety of travel options based on your budget. Accommodation might cost between €30 and €50 per night for affordable alternatives and more than €200 for luxury lodgings. A lunch at a basic restaurant costs between €10 and €20, whereas premium ones cost more than €50. In Lyon, public transit costs about €1.90 each ticket, while vehicle rentals start around €30 per day.

2. Currency and Payment Options: The native currency is the euro (€). Credit and debit cards are frequently accepted; however, smaller

establishments may require cash. ATMs are widely available, and many machines provide instructions in multiple languages.

3. Accommodation Costs: Budget hotels and hostels range from €30 to €50 per night.

Mid-range hotels and guesthouses: €70–€120 per night.

Luxury hotels cost over €200 per night.

Consider reserving ahead of time and searching for specials on travel websites to get the best rates.

4. Food and Dining Expenses: Casual meals range from €10 to €20.

Mid-range restaurants cost between €25 and €40.

Fine dining costs more than €50.

Save money by going to local markets, where you can get fresh food and ready-to-eat meals at low costs.

5. Transportation Costs: Public transportation (bus, tram, subway) costs €1.90 per ticket, with

possibilities for day passes.

Car rentals start at €30 per day.

Fuel expenses are between €1.50-€2 per liter.

Consider obtaining inexpensive passes if you frequently travel within cities.

6. Activity and Attraction Costs: Museum entry fees range from €5 to €15.

Guided trips cost €20-€50.

Outdoor activities (such as wine tours and hiking): Prices vary, and some are free.

Look for free or reduced-cost activities, such as walking tours or free museum days.

7. Budgeting Tip: Plan your spending in advance and create a daily budget.

Use travel apps to keep track of your expenditures and identify beneficial offers.

To get reduced pricing, book your lodgings and transportation early.

8. Money-Saving Strategies: Travel off-season for reduced pricing and fewer crowds.

Reserve your lodging and transportation in

advance.

Take advantage of local markets for cheap meals and souvenirs.

Consider staying in low-cost accommodations such as hostels or guesthouses.

Use public transit instead of taxis or auto rentals whenever possible.

Chapter Two

Top Attractions

Historic Sites

The Rhone region boasts numerous historical sites that reflect its rich history and cultural heritage. From ancient Roman theaters to enormous cathedrals, majestic castles, and instructive museums, the region has something for everyone, whether they are history buffs or casual visitors.

Roman Theater of Orange: The Roman Theater of

Orange, a UNESCO World Heritage site, is one

of the most well-preserved Roman theaters in the world, dating back to the first century AD. It is well-known for its amazing size and acoustic properties. The theater is located at Rue madeleine and can be reached by phone at +33 4 90 51 17 60.

The Ancient Theater of Fourvière in Lyon

This theater was built in the 15th century BC as part of the Roman colony of Lugdunum. It provides panoramic views of Lyon and hosts the annual Nuits de Fourvière festival. You can find the theater at 17 Rue Cleberg, 69005 Lyon, and call them at +33 4 72 38 49 30.

Historical Significance: These theaters were important social and cultural institutions in Roman times, holding a wide range of acts and public gatherings. Their preservation provides insight into past architectural prowess and cultural traditions.

Visitor Information

Roman Theater of Orange: Every day from 9am - 7pm, the entrance fee is approximately €9.50. It offers guided tours and sponsors events such as the Chorégies d'Orange opera festival.

Ancient Theatre of Fourvière: Open daily, with an entrance fee of approximately €4. It offers guided tours and organizes performances as part of the Nuits de Fourvière festival.

Cathedrals and Churches

Lyon Cathedral: This Gothic cathedral in Lyon, also known as Saint Jean Baptiste Cathedral, dates back to the 12th century and boasts an astronomical clock from the 14th century.

Basilica of Notre-Dame de Fourvière: Perched atop Fourvière Hill, Situated at 8 Plaza de fourvière, 69005 Lyon and can be contacted at +33 4 78 25 13 01, this basilica provides breathtaking views of Lyon.

It was built in the late nineteenth century and mixes Romanesque and Byzantine architecture.

Lyon Cathedral's architectural features include elaborate Gothic architecture, stained glass windows, and an astronomical clock.

The Basilica of Notre-Dame de Fourvière is known for its intricate internal mosaics, breathtaking stained glass, and panoramic views.

Visitor Information

Lyon Cathedral: Open daily except on Mondays from 9am - 12pm, 2pm - 6:30pm and free admission. Donations are appreciated. Guided tours are offered.

Basilica of Notre-Dame de Fourvière: Open daily with hours of operation are 7am to 9pm, with a latest closing time of 10pm, free admission. Donations are appreciated. Guided tours are offered. Attend Mass or a special service.

Castles and Palaces

Palais des Papes at Avignon It was one of

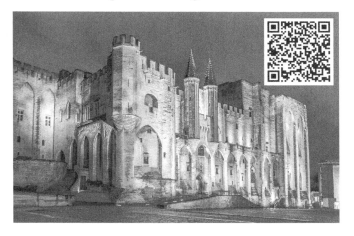

Europe's largest and most important medieval Gothic buildings, serving as the papal palace in the 14th century. It is located at PL. du Palais, 84000, Avignon.

Château de Crussol: A medieval stronghold overlooking the Rhône Valley that provides picturesque vistas and historical context. Situated at Chem. de beauregard, 07130 saint-peray.

Historical Significance: In the 14th century, the Palais des Papes represented the papacy's political influence. Château de Crussol offers insight into medieval defense architecture and feudal history.

Visitor Information

Palais des Papes: Open daily from 9am to 7pm, with an entrance fee of approximately €12.

Guided tours and audio guides are available. You can also get to them by calling +33 4 32 74 32 74.

Château de Crussol: Open daily, free admission. Guided tours are available upon request. Phone: +33 4 75 81 00 51

Museums and Historical Exhibits

Musée des Confluences in Lyon:Located at 86 Quai Perrache, is a revolutionary science center and anthropological museum that embodies the fusion of sciences and society. Its breathtaking modern architecture, a symphony of steel, glass, and a shimmering white concrete, sets the tone for an immersive experience that explores the intersection of human knowledge and innovation. Through its captivating exhibits and interactive displays, the museum explores the intricacies of our world inviting visitors to ponder the intricate relationships between science, technology, and humanity.

Museum of Fine Arts of Lyon: One of France's largest art museums, located in a former Benedictine abbey (20 Pl. des Terreaux, 69001) Collections and Exhibits: The Musée des Confluences showcases natural history, anthropology, and science collections. Lyon's Museum of Fine Arts has large collections of paintings, sculptures, and

decorative arts dating back to ancient Egypt and modern times.

Visitor Information

Musée des Confluences: Open Tuesday-Sunday from 10:30am to 6:30pm, entry fee is approximately €9. Guided tours and special exhibitions are available. You can get through them by calling +33 4 28 12 12

Museum of Fine Arts of Lyon: Open Wednesday to Monday from 10 am to 6 pm, with an entrance fee of approximately €8. Guided tours and special exhibitions are available. For more assistance contact them at +33 4 72 10 17 40

Archaeological Sites

Vienne: Famous for its Roman ruins, notably  the Temple of Augustus and Livia and the Roman Theater.

Glanum: An old Roman city near

Saint-Rémy-de-Provence with well-preserved remains.

Historic Significance: Vienne's Roman ruins demonstrate the city's significance during the Roman Empire. Glanum provides insight into the daily life and architecture of an ancient Roman city.

Visitor Information

Vienne: Open daily and offers combined ticket choices for multiple locations. Guided tours are offered.

Glanum: Open daily, with an entrance fee of roughly €8. Guided tours are offered.

Additional Historic Landmarks

Pont Saint-Bénézet in Avignon: A well-known medieval bridge.

Tarascon defenses: medieval defenses that have been well preserved.

Historical Context: Pont Saint-Bénézet is a

landmark in Avignon with a rich history based on local traditions.

Tarascon's defenses represent medieval military architecture.

Visitor information

Pont Saint-Bénézet: Open daily, with an entrance fee of roughly €5. Guided tours are offered.

Fortifications of Tarascon: Open every day, with an admission charge of around €6. Guided tours are offered.

Insider Tips and Recommendations

Best Times to Visit: To avoid crowds, visit early in the morning or late in the afternoon. Weekdays are typically less busy than weekends.

Special Event: Look for special events, like reenactments, festivals, or night excursions, that might offer a one-of-a-kind experience.

Natural Wonders

The Rhone region has a variety of natural wonders, including the renowned river, wineries, national parks, and breathtaking scenery. This diverse region provides stunning landscapes and a plethora of outdoor activities for nature lovers and adventurers alike.

Rhône River

The Rhône River is a prominent watercourse that flows through the region, playing an important role in its nature, history, and economics. It runs from the Swiss Alps to southeastern France and into the Mediterranean Sea, enhancing the landscapes it crosses.

Scenic Spots: The riverbanks in Lyon provide magnificent vistas of the city and active riverfront districts.

The vineyards of Côtes du Rhône, where the river feeds some of the world's most famous vineyards.

The Camargue delta is famous for its unique wetlands, diversified animals, and breathtaking natural beauty.

Activities: River cruises are a peaceful way to explore the region's highlights.

Kayaking and canoeing for adventurous people.

Beautiful walking and cycling lanes along the riverfront.

Visitor Information

The best seasons to visit are spring and autumn, which have milder weather and fewer tourists.

Guided tours and river cruises are provided all year, including exceptional events such as Lyon's Fête des Lumières in December.

National and Regional Parks

Parc Naturel Régional du Pilat: Includes different landscapes like forests, vineyards, and mountains.

Popular hiking trails include treks to Mont Pilat, which provide panoramic views.

Camargue Natural Park is known for its unique wetlands, pink flamingos, and wild horses.

Activities include bird watching, horseback riding, and exploring the salt flats.

Visitor Information

Both parks are open year-round and have no entrance costs.

Guided tours and special programs are available for further exploration.

Scenic scenery

Monts d'Ardèche: Known for its volcanic scenery, rivers, and deep forests.

Gorges de l'Ardèche: Stunning gorges with kayaking, hiking, and breathtaking views.

Beaujolais Hills: Beautiful undulating hills with vineyards and quaint communities.

Visitor Information

Local tourism offices provide information on the best routes and seasonal attractions.

Some regions may demand permits or entrance fees for certain activities.

Lakes and Waterfalls

Lac du Bourget, France's largest natural lake, ideal for boating, swimming, and picnicking.
Cascade du Ray-Pic is a magnificent waterfall in Ardèche that is best viewed in the spring or early summer.

Visitor Information

Accessibility varies; some locations may require a short hike.
Picnic sites, cafes, and visitor centers can be found nearby.

Flora and Fauna

Unique Species: The Camargue has several unique species, including the Camargue horse and other bird species.
Natural Trails: Numerous trails provide

opportunities to discover the region's biodiversity.

Guided wildlife expeditions are available in places like the Camargue and Pilat.

Visitor Information

The best periods for animal observation are early morning and late afternoon.

Following marked trails and respecting local wildlife are precautions to take.

Insider Tips and Recommendations

Best Time to Visit: Spring and autumn provide favorable weather and fewer tourists.

Summer is perfect for river activities and vineyard tours, while winter brings special events such as the Fête des Lumières.

Photography Tip: Capture golden hour light along the Rhône River.

Use a zoom lens to shoot wildlife in the Camargue.

Cultural Landmark

The Rhone region has numerous cultural landmarks, including a strong arts scene and rich historical legacy. From renowned museums and art galleries to historical and cultural centers, the region has a wide range of attractions for culture lovers.

Museums

The Gallo-Roman Museum (Musée Gallo-Romain de Lyon-Fourvière) has the following description:

This museum is dedicated to Lyon's Roman history and provides a fascinating peek into the ancient city of Lugdunum through its collection of antiquities.

Key exhibits include Roman mosaics, sculptures, and everyday objects.

Models and reconstructions of old Roman structures.

Interactive exhibits and educational activities.

Visitor information
Open Tuesday through Sunday, 10:00 a.m. to 6:00 p.m. Closed on Mondays.
Entrance fees are €7 for adults, €4 for students, and free for children under 18.
Guided tours are available; visit the museum's website for schedules.
Special events and educational sessions take place on a regular basis.

Art galleries
Musée d'Art Contemporain de Lyon (MAC Lyon): This contemporary art museum (Address: Cité Internationale, 81 Quai Charles de Gaulle, 69006) is known for its creative exhibitions and installations, showcasing works by prominent and new artists.
Key Exhibits: recognized contemporary artists and current shows.

Exhibits showcase current trends and themes in contemporary art.

Visitor Information

Open Wednesday-Sunday from 11:00 a.m. to 6:00 p.m. Closed Mondays and Tuesdays. Entrance fees are €8 for adults, €4 for students, and free for children under 18. Guided tours and workshops are offered; see the museum's website for dates. Phone: +33 4 72 69 17 17

Galerie Le Réverbère (Lyon): This gallery (Address: 38 Rue Burdeau, 69001) focuses on modern photography, showcasing works by famous photographers and hosting exhibitions that push the medium's frontiers.

Featured Artists: Highlight significant photographers and exhibits that have been featured.

Visitor Information

Hours of operation: Wednesday-Saturday, 2:00-7:00 p.m.

Admission Fees: Free.

Special events and exhibitions are routinely held. Phone: +33 4 72 00 06 72

Historical and Cultural Centers

Centre d'Histoire de la Résistance et de la Déportation (Lyon): This museum (Address: 14 Av. Berthelot, 69007), dedicated to the history of the French Resistance during World War II, provides a poignant and informative experience.

Key Exhibits include personal testimony, papers, and artifacts from the resistance.

Interactive displays and multimedia presentations.

Visitor information

Open Wednesday through Sunday, 10:00 a.m. to 6:00 p.m. Closed on Mondays and Tuesdays.

Entrance fees are €6 for adults, €4 for students, and free for children under 18.

Guided tours are available; visit the museum's website for schedules.

Special events and educational programs are often held. Phone: +33 4 72 73 99 00

Institut Lumière (Lyon): This museum (Rue du Premier Film, 69008) honors the Lumière brothers, cinema pioneers, and commemorates film's invention and history.

Key Exhibits include early film equipment and historical items.

Classic cinema screenings and educational events.

Visitor Information

Open Tuesday-Sunday, 10:00 AM-6:00 PM. Closed on Mondays.

Entrance fees are €8 for adults, €6 for students and seniors, and free for children under 18.

Guided tours are available; visit the museum's website for schedules.

Special programs and film screenings take place on a regular basis. Phone: +33 4 78 78 18 95

Theatre and Performance Venues

Théâtre des Célestins (Lyon): This historic theater (4 Rue Charles Dullin, 69002) is noted for its classical and modern productions, offering a broad program of performances.

Programs and Shows: Upcoming performances, such as plays, concerts, and special events.

Visitor Information

Office hours: Tuesday through Saturday, 12:00 PM to 7:00 PM.

Ticket prices vary for each show; visit the theater's website for more information or call +33 4 72 77 40 00.

Guided tours are available; see the theater's website for schedules.

The Lyon Opera House (Opéra Nouvel) is known for its modern architecture and wide performance schedule, including opera, ballet, and concerts.

Programs and Shows include current and forthcoming performances.

Visitor Information

It is situated at 1 Pl. de la Comédie, 69001.

Office hours: Tuesday through Saturday, 12:00 PM to 7:00 PM.

Ticket prices vary by show; visit the opera house's website for more information or call +33 4 69 85 54 54

Guided tours are available; see the opera house's website for schedules.

Local Artists and Workshops

The Rhone region boasts numerous local artisans and workshops where visitors may observe traditional crafts and purchase unique gifts.

Artists and workshops are available throughout the region, especially in Lyon and smaller towns.

Opening hours vary by workshop; check local listings for further information.

Some seminars offer special tours and hands-on learning opportunities.

Insider Tips and Recommendations

Best Time to Visit: Spring and autumn for milder weather and fewer tourists.

Summer is the season for outdoor festivals and cultural activities.

Indoor exhibitions and celebratory events, such as Lyon's Fête des Lumières, take place during the winter.

Special Events and Festivals: Keep an eye out for any special events or temporary exhibitions that may overlap with your visit.

For low-cost trips, take advantage of free admission days at museums and galleries.

Modern Attractions

The Rhone area expertly integrates its rich historical past with modernity, providing a variety of contemporary attractions highlighting creative architecture, cutting-edge art, and bustling urban developments. Visitors can experience a broad range of modern landmarks, cultural places, commercial districts, and culinary delights.

Modern architecture and landmarks
Tour Oxygène (Lyon): Tour Oxygène is a 115-meter-tall skyscraper in Lyon Part-Dieu

commercial area (10-12 boulevard Vivier-Merle - 69003)

Significance: The skyscraper is a prominent component of Lyon's skyline, housing office spaces, retail facilities, and a panoramic observation deck with excellent views of the city.

Visitor Information

Access: Public areas, including the shopping mall at the base.

Opening hours: Monday to Friday by 7:30 am till 7pm.

There is no entrance fee for public places; however, certain excursions or events may require one.

Modern Art and Cultural Spaces

La Sucrière (Lyon): La Sucrière (49-50 Quai Rambaud, 69002), a modern art space housed in a former sugar factory, serves as a center for artistic innovation and creation.

Events and Exhibits: hosts significant art exhibitions, including the Biennale de Lyon.

Visitor Information

Opening hours vary per event; refer to the venue's website for specifics.

Entrance fees vary by exhibition.

Special events and programs are often held.

Science and Innovation Centers

Cité du Design (3 Rue Javelin Pagnon, 42000 Saint-Étienne): This center promotes design and innovation through exhibitions, workshops, and educational programs showcasing cutting-edge technology.

Key Exhibitions are exhibitions on sustainable design, technological innovation, and modern design approaches.

Visitor Information

Open Tuesday-Sunday 10:00 AM-6:00 PM. Closed on Mondays.

Entrance fees are €6 for adults, €4 for students, and free for children under 18.

Guided tours and workshops are available; see the center's website for schedules or call +33 4 77 49 74 70.

NOTE: The Cité du design is closed from July 14 to August 26, 2024, and reopens on September 20, 2024, with a new program. It is part of the EPCC, a platform combining education, research, and promotion of design and art. Located in the former Saint-Étienne Arms Factory, it unites the Cité du design and the École supérieure d'art et design.

Lyon Confluence is a sustainable and modern urban renewal project that has transformed an outdated industrial area into a bustling zone.

Attractions: Highlights include the Confluence

shopping area, unique residential buildings, public spaces, and cultural venues.

Visitor Information

Accessible via public transit. Guided tours are available; see local listings for schedules. Special events and activities are often held in the neighborhood.

Retail and Entertainment Districts

La Part-Dieu (Lyon): La Part-Dieu, a significant commercial and business district, is recognized for its numerous retail malls, entertainment alternatives, and contemporary infrastructure.

Key Attractions: One of Europe's largest shopping malls, Part-Dieu, has theaters, restaurants, and cafes.

Visitor Information

The shopping center is open daily from 9:00 AM to 8:00 PM.

Transportation: Public transportation is well connected.

Special events and promotions are routinely held.

Les Halles de Lyon

Paul Bocuse: This sophisticated food market, named after the legendary chef Paul Bocuse, is a gourmet's dream, featuring a diverse selection of high-quality foods.

Highlights: Lyon's gastronomic legacy is highlighted by renowned food merchants and gourmet items and dining alternatives.

Visitor Information

Opening hours: Tuesday-Saturday, 7:00 AM-10:30 PM; Sunday, 7:00 AM- 4:30 PM; closed on Mondays.

Location: centrally placed, with excellent access to public transportation.

Special events and tastings are regularly held.

Parks and Public Space

Parc de la Tête d'Or (Lyon): This wide urban park is a green oasis in the center of Lyon, famed for its stunning botanical gardens, calm lake, and family-friendly zoo.

Modern amenities include playgrounds, boating facilities, bicycle trails, and sports spaces.

Visitor information

Open daily from sunrise to sunset.

Entrance costs are free; however, some attractions within the park may demand money.

Special events and programs are often hosted.

Parc Blandan (Lyon) is a recently rebuilt urban park with modern design and vast leisure facilities.

Highlights: Notable amenities include sports facilities, playgrounds, skate parks, and public art works.

Visitor Information

Open daily from sunrise to dusk. conveniently placed near the city's core. Special events and activities are routinely scheduled.

Modern gastronomy

The Rhone region is home to a variety of innovative restaurants that offer modern cuisine and distinctive dining experiences.

Le Kitchen Café (Lyon): Known for its innovative cuisine and cozy setting.

Prairial (Lyon): recognized for its contemporary, seasonal cuisine and sophisticated presentation.

Visitor information

Reservations are recommended for most major restaurants.

Prices range from moderate to high, depending on the establishment.

Special Dining Experiences: Look for tasting menus and chef specials.

Winter offers a pleasant interior atmosphere and festive activities.

Special Events and Festivals: Check local listings for events like the Biennale de Lyon, Fête des Lumières, and temporary exhibitions.

Local insights: Take advantage of free or discounted admission days at some museums and cultural institutions.

Chapter Three

Things to Do

Outdoor Activities

The Rhone region's diversified landscape provides a variety of outdoor activities. Every adventurer will find something to enjoy, from trekking through volcanic peaks and lovely villages to cycling through vineyards and along rivers. Whether you choose high-adrenaline sports or peaceful activities, the Rhone region's natural splendor and many outdoor experiences will enchant you.

Hiking

Popular Hiking Trails

Sentier du Rhône: This long-distance trail follows the Rhône River, affording spectacular views and the opportunity to discover the river's natural and cultural history. The scenic areas near Lyon, as well as the more difficult roads in the Ardèche, are particularly noteworthy.

The Monts d'Ardèche Regional Nature Park: This park is famous for its volcanic peaks, deep woods, and picturesque settlements. Popular routes include trails to the Gerbier de Jonc and Mont Mézenc, which provide panoramic vistas and insight into the region's geological history.

The pilgrimage route to Mont Saint-Romain is both a physical challenge and a cultural trip. The walk takes you past vineyards, Romanesque cathedrals, and other historical sites before ending at the peak of Mont Saint-Romain.

Difficulty Level

Easy: Sentier du Rhône (near Lyon), family-friendly routes in the Monts d'Ardèche.

Moderate: pilgrimage route to Mont Saint-Romain, with mid-level trails in the

Ardèche.

Difficult: high-altitude paths in the Monts d'Ardèche and lengthier stretches of the Sentier du Rhône.

Guided Hikes are available from local tour companies and national park visitor centers. Guides give historical context, natural insights, and ensure safety.

Visitor information

The best seasons for pleasant weather are spring and autumn, while summer offers rich scenery.

Supplies include sturdy hiking boots, water, maps, and sun protection.

Permits are generally not necessary, but verify local rules in certain places.

Cycling

Popular Cycling Routes

ViaRhôna: This long-distance cycling route connects Lake Geneva to the Mediterranean

Sea. The Rhone region's key components include attractive roads through Lyon and picturesque countryside expanses.

Beaujolais Wine Journey: A lovely journey through the undulating vineyards of Beaujolais, with stops at wineries to try local wines.

Lyon City Cycling: Lyon's large network of bike lanes and pathways along the Rhône and Saône rivers provide an excellent way to explore the city.

Bike Rental and Tours: Available from a variety of providers in Lyon and surrounding towns. Guided tours provide insights into the local history and culture.

Visitor Information

Safety: Wear helmets, obey traffic laws, and remain hydrated.

Equipment: comfortable riding attire, water, and route maps.

Boating

Boat Tours and Cruises

Rhône River Cruises: Options include picturesque sightseeing cruises, dinner cruises, and multi-day itineraries to discover the Rhône's beauty and history.

Lyon Boat Cruises: Short cruises that showcase Lyon's architecture, bridges, and riverside sites.

Ardèche Gorges Canoeing: Canoeing and kayaking in the Ardèche Gorges is an exciting way to explore the spectacular limestone canyons.

Sailing and Yachting: Available on the Rhône River and neighboring lakes, including rentals and instruction from local sailing schools.

Visitor information

Reservations can be made online or at local tourism offices.

Prices vary according to tour length and type.

Safety: Follow the guide's advice and wear a life jacket.

Other Outdoor Activities

Rock Climbing: Popular areas include the limestone cliffs of the Vercors and the stunning crags of the Ardèche.

Paragliding: The region's takeoff points offer stunning vistas and thrilling experiences, including courses and tandem flights.

Fishing: The Rhône River and nearby lakes are famous for fishing; make sure you have the proper licenses.

Golf: Notable courses include Golf de Lyon and Golf du Beaujolais, which provide superb amenities and stunning scenery.

Seasonal Activity

Winter Sports: The adjacent French Alps offer chances for skiing, snowboarding, and snowshoeing.

Water Sports: Popular summer activities include paddleboarding, windsurfing, and jet skiing on surrounding lakes and rivers.

Family-Friendly Outdoor Activities

Nature Parks and Reserves: Lyon's Parc de la Tête d'Or offers family-friendly activities like simple paths, picnic spots, and educational programs.

Adventure Parks: Parks such as France Aventures in Lyon provide zip-lining, rope courses, and climbing walls for people of all ages.

Cultural Activities

The Rhone area boasts a rich heritage, gastronomic traditions, and bustling festival scene. There are several possibilities to immerse oneself in local culture, ranging from cooking classes that teach the art of Lyonnaise cuisine to exciting festivals that celebrate music, lighting, and gastronomy. To properly understand the Rhone's unique cultural fabric, participate in artistic workshops and take guided tours of historical places.

Cooking Classes

Lyon Culinary Institute: Provides classes on traditional Lyonnaise cuisine, including classic dishes and pastry-making workshops.

Classes are held on a regular basis. Prices range between €50 and €150 for every class. Reservations can be made online, and sessions are taught in French with English translation available.

Beaujolais Wine and Cooking School offers cooking workshops and wine tastings, with a focus on regional delicacies.

Classes include wine tastings. Prices start at €75. Classes are offered in both French and

English.

Market to Table Classes: Participants will tour local markets, such as Les Halles de Lyon Paul Bocuse, to select fresh ingredients for cooking. Classes typically take place in the morning. Prices range between €60 and €120. It is advised that you book in advance. Participants may expect hands-on training, take-home recipes, and, on occasion, exceptional guest chefs from well-known local restaurants.

Festival

Major Festivals

Fête des Lumières (event of Lights, Lyon): Held in December, this event showcases dazzling light displays, art installations, and cultural performances across the city.

Visitor Information: The festival is completely free to attend. Due to the huge number of visitors, it is recommended that you reserve your accommodations in advance.

Nuits Sonores (Lyon) is an electronic music festival with significant performances, varied locations, and cultural events.

Visitor information: Held in May. Ticket prices vary from €30 to €150, depending on the event. Tickets can be bought online.

Les Nuits de Fourvière (Lyon) is a summer event held at the Roman Theatre of Fourvière, featuring music, theater, dance, and circus performances.

Visitor Information: Open from June to August. Ticket costs range from €20 to €80. It is advised that you book in advance.

Local Festivals

Wine Harvest Festivals (Various Locations): Traditional celebrations in Beaujolais and Côtes du Rhône areas, incorporating wine tastings, parades, and local cuisine.

Visitor Information: Typically held between September and October. Entry fees vary, and certain events are free.

Gastronomy Festivals: Events such as the Lyon International Fair and Beaujolais Nouveau festivals highlight regional cuisine and culinary innovation.

Visitor Information: The dates and entry prices change. Check local listings for specific event information.

Arts and Crafts Workshops

Pottery and Ceramics: Learn traditional pottery techniques and create your own pieces.

Visitor Information: Workshops are held on a weekly basis. Prices vary from €30 to €100. Booking is required.

Textile and Weaving Workshops: Learn traditional textile techniques, such as silk weaving, in Lyon.

Visitor Information: Classes are offered periodically. Prices start at €50. You can make reservations online.

Painting and Drawing Classes: Learn to capture the landscapes and urban settings of the Rhone area.

Visitor Information: Classes are offered throughout the year. Prices vary from €40 to €120. Materials are frequently supplied.

History and Culture Tours

Lyon Old Town (Vieux Lyon): Walking tours of the UNESCO World Heritage site, highlighting Renaissance architecture and historical landmarks.

Visitor Information: Tours are offered daily. Prices vary from €15 to €30. Meeting spots are typically located in central Lyon.

Wine Tours: Guided tours of the Beaujolais and Côtes du Rhône areas, with vineyard visits and tastings.

Visitor Information: Full-day trips cost €75. It is advised that you book in advance.

Historical Sites: Tours of important sites, including the Roman Theatre of Fourvière and the medieval town of Pérouges.

Visitor Info: Prices range from €20 to €50. For timetables, check with local tour providers.

Self-Guided Tours: Use apps, maps, and suggested itineraries to explore at your leisure.

Visitor Information: There are many tours available to download online. Prices vary from free to a modest price.

Music & Dance

Live Music Venues include classical concerts at the Lyon Opera House and contemporary performances at local bars.

Visitor information: The performance schedule and ticket pricing have changed. Booking online is frequently accessible.

Local Marketplaces and Fairs

Market Experiences: Visit local markets, such as Les Halles de Lyon Paul Bocuse, to find fresh vegetables, gourmet delicacies, and artisan products.

Visitor Information: Markets are usually open daily. Check the local listings for exact hours and events.

Seasonal craft fairs offer visitors the opportunity to purchase handmade goods and mementos.

Visitor Information: The dates and venues vary. Entry is frequently free.

Family-Friendly Activities

The Rhone region provides a diverse choice of activities for families and children of all ages. There are numerous options to keep everyone entertained and engaged, including huge parks and interactive museums, as well as animal encounters and adventure parks. Whether you like outdoor adventures or cultural encounters, the Rhone area is an excellent choice for family enjoyment.

Parks and Playgrounds

Parc de la Tête d'Or (Lyon): This huge urban park is a green paradise in the center of Lyon, containing botanical gardens, a zoo, a tranquil lake, and extensive playgrounds.

Activities: Families can go boating on the lake, visit the zoo, picnic, and play on the playground.

Visitor Information: Open everyday from 6:30 a.m. to 10:30 p.m. Entry is free; however, certain attractions, such as boat rentals, require a cost. There are bathrooms, picnic spaces, and eateries.

Parc Blandan (Lyon): A modern urban park with historical features and contemporary design, including play areas, sports facilities, and open spaces.

Activities include cycling, sports, outdoor events, and exploring the unique playgrounds.

Visitor information: Open everyday from 6:30 a.m. to 10:30 p.m. Entry is free. There are bathrooms, picnic spots, and sports equipment rentals available.

Educative and Interactive Museums

The Musée des Confluences (Lyon) is a science and anthropology museum with interactive displays that appeal to both children and adults.

Highlights: Key exhibits include dinosaur skeletons, natural history displays, and interactive activities for children.

Visitor information: Open Tuesday through Sunday, 10 a.m. to 6 p.m. Admission is €9 for adults, €6 for children aged 18-25, and free for children under 18. Guided tours and family activities are available.

Mini World Lyon: A miniature park with precise models of cities, landscapes, and animated sceneries that provide a fantastic experience for youngsters.

Activities include interactive displays, special events, and themed sections where miniatures come to life.

Visitor information: Open every day from 10 a.m. to 7 p.m. Admission is €14 for adults, €10 for children aged 4 to 12, and free for children under four. There's a gift shop and a café.

Animal encounters and farming

Zoo de Lyon (Parc de la Tête d'Or): This zoo, located in Parc de la Tête d'Or, houses a broad selection of species from around the world.

Activities: Animal feedings, educational events, and special exhibits all make an enjoyable experience for families.

Visitor information: Open everyday from 9 a.m. to 5:30 p.m. Entry is free. There are bathrooms, eateries, and picnic spots.

Visit local farms and petting zoos to interact with animals and learn about agricultural life.

Activities: Hands-on activities include animal feeding, farm tours, and seasonal events such as pumpkin picking and hayrides.

Visitor information: Locations and hours vary. The typical opening hours are 10 a.m. to 6 p.m. Admission fees range between €5 and €15. It is advised that you book in advance.

Amusement and adventure parks

Walibi Rhône-Alpes: A family-friendly amusement park with thrilling rides, shows, and attractions.

Highlights: Popular rides, family-friendly attractions, and seasonal events make it a must-see destination for families.

Visitor information: Open from April to November. Admission is €32 for adults, €28 for children aged 3 to 11, and free for children under three. There are restaurants, bathrooms, and picnic spots.

France Aventures (Lyon): An adventure park that offers zip lines, rope courses, and climbing sports for all ages.

Activity: Courses built for various skill levels and ages ensure that the entire family has fun and stays safe.

Visitor information: Open every day from 10 a.m. to 6 p.m. Admission: €25 for adults, €20 for children aged 6 to 12, and €15 for children under 6. Safety equipment is supplied, and previous reservations are recommended.

Family-Friendly Cultural Activities

Theatre and Puppet Shows: Family-friendly performances, such as puppet shows and children's theater, are available at theaters and cultural centers.

Highlights: Popular events and performances are geared for younger audiences, making cultural vacations entertaining for the entire family.

Visitor Information: Schedules and ticket costs differ. It is recommended that you book in advance, especially for popular performances.

Family-friendly festivals and events include music festivals, outdoor film evenings, and holiday celebrations.

Activities: Children-friendly activities like face painting, crafts, and interactive exhibitions guarantee that everyone has a positive time.

Visitor Information: The dates, venues, and

admission costs change. Restrooms, food kiosks, and picnic spots are common amenities.

Nightlife and Entertainment

The Rhone region offers a diverse range of entertainment options to satisfy all tastes. Whether you want to dance the night away at a busy nightclub, relax with a handmade cocktail at a fashionable bar, or see live music and cultural acts, the Rhone region has something for everyone.

Nightclubs and Dance Venues

Le Sucre (Lyon): This rooftop nightclub is known for its electronic music, panoramic city views, and themed parties, making it a popular place for nightlife enthusiasts.

Ninkasi Gerland (Lyon): A multifunctional venue that mixes a nightclub, live music, and a craft brewery to provide a distinctive and dynamic entertainment experience.

Ayers Rock Boat (Lyon): A floating nightclub on the Rhône River famous for its lively atmosphere, themed events, and breathtaking waterfront views.

Music Genres: These venues cater to a wide range of musical preferences, including electronic, hip-hop, pop, and rock.

Visitor Information

Le Sucre is open Friday to Sunday from 11 PM to 6 AM. Entrance prices normally range from €10 to €20. Dress code: casual chic. Reserve VIP tables in advance.

Ninkasi Gerland is open daily from 10 a.m. until 2 a.m. Entrance costs vary. There is no rigorous dress code.

Ayers Rock Boat: Open Wednesday through Saturday, 10 p.m. to 4 a.m. Entrance costs vary.

Dress code: casual. Reserve VIP tables in advance.

Bars and Pubs

Le Fantôme de l'Opéra (Lyon): This bar is known for its innovative drinks and trendy design, providing a fashionable and sophisticated ambiance.

Antiquaire (Lyon): A speakeasy-style bar with classic cocktails and a retro environment, ideal for a relaxing evening.

Les Fleurs du Malt (Lyon): A popular beer pub with a diverse selection of craft beers and a relaxed ambiance, perfect for beer lovers.

Rooftop Bars: Rooftop bars such as Le Sucre and Celeste Bar provide breathtaking views of the city, making for an unforgettable evening out.

Visitor Information

Le Fantôme de l'Opéra is open daily from 6 PM to 2 AM. Cocktails cost €10-€15. Happy hour: 6 to 8 p.m.

Antiquaire is open daily from 5 p.m. until 2 a.m. Cocktails cost €10-€15. Booking is recommended for weekends.

Les Fleurs du Malt is open daily from 4 p.m. until 1 a.m. Craft beers range from €5 to €8. Special events include weekly beer tastings.

Live Music Venues

Transbordeur (Lyon): An iconic concert venue featuring a variety of music genres from rock to electronic, attracting both local and worldwide musicians.

La Marquise (Lyon): A tiny live music venue on a barge recognized for its diverse schedule of artists and distinctive surroundings.

Radiant-Bellevue (Caluire-et-Cuire): A popular concert theater that accommodates a diverse range of concerts, including worldwide performers and local bands.

Jazz Clubs: Jazz fans will appreciate locations such as Hot Club de Lyon, which is noted for its warm atmosphere and live jazz performances.

Visitor Information
Transbordeur: Show schedules and ticket pricing can vary. Purchase tickets in advance online.

La Marquise: Open Thursday through Sunday, 8 p.m. to 2 a.m. Show tickets cost between €10 and €20. Book online.

Radiant-Bellevue: The performance schedule and ticket pricing have changed. Purchase tickets in advance online.

Theaters and Cultural Performances
Théâtre des Célestins (Lyon): A historic theater with classic and current plays, providing a rich cultural experience.

Opéra de Lyon: The opera house provides a range of acts, including opera, ballet, and classical concerts, which draw cultural lovers.

Cultural Events: Seasonal cultural events and performances, including the Nuits de Fourvière festival, offer a variety of entertainment options.

Visitor Information

Theatre des Célestins: Performance schedules and ticket pricing may vary. Purchase tickets in advance online.

Opéra de Lyon: The performance schedule and ticket pricing fluctuate. Purchase tickets in advance online.

Cinema and Outdoor Movies

UGC Ciné Cité Confluence (Lyon): A modern cinema complex with a diverse selection of films and excellent seats, ideal for moviegoers.

Outdoor Movie Nights: During the summer, outdoor movie screenings at venues such as

Parc de la Tête d'Or offer a lovely experience beneath the stars.

Visitor Information

UGC Ciné Cité Confluence is open daily. Ticket prices range from €10 to €15. Special screenings and events.

Outdoor Movie Nights are typically conducted in the summer. Check the local listings for timetables and locations. Entry is free or has minor expenses.

Late-Night Dining and Food Markets

Bouchons Lyonnais: Traditional Lyonnaise eateries serving hearty meals late into the night, ideal for a late-night dining experience.

Food Trucks: Popular food trucks and street food sellers, such as those at the Marche Gare food market, are open in the evenings and offer a variety of delectable choices.

Night Markets: Night markets have a diverse

range of food stalls and local delicacies, providing a lively and bustling scene.

Visitor Information

Bouchons Lyonnais: Open late, usually till midnight or later. Reservations are recommended.

Food Trucks: Open hours vary. Check the local listings for locations and times.

Night Markets: Dates and hours vary. Check your local listings for further information.

New Nighttime Experiences

Night excursions: Evening river excursions on the Rhône and Saône provide a new perspective of the city at night, including dinner and sightseeing.

Ghost Tours: Spooky evening tours explore Lyon's ghostly history and folklore, providing an exciting experience for paranormal enthusiasts.

Visitor Information

Night Cruises: Prices and itineraries may vary. Book in advance online or at a local tourist bureau.

Ghost Tours: costs and timing vary. Book in advance online or at a local tourist bureau. Recommended for ages 12 and older.

Chapter Three

Food and Drink

Traditional cuisine and regional specialties

The Rhone area is known for its rich culinary legacy, which combines ancient recipes with local products to create a variety of tasty dishes. Influenced by its historical links and geographical diversity, Rhone cuisine offers a distinct blend of rustic and sophisticated flavors, making it a foodie's dream.

Traditional Dishes

Salade Lyonnaise: This famous Lyonnaise salad  is created with frisée lettuce, crispy bacon, poached eggs, and croutons.

It is typically topped with a tangy mustard vinaigrette.

Recommended Restaurants: For a typical Salade Lyonnaise, visit Café des Fédérations or Bouchon des Cordeliers, both known for their authentic Lyonnaise food.

Quenelles de Brochet: Delicious Lyonnaise pike  dumplings served with crayfish or béchamel sauce.

Recommended Restaurants: Try Quenelles de Brochet at La Mère Brazier or Daniel & Denise, both of which are well-known for their mastery of this dish.

Cervelle de Canut is a traditional Lyonnaise

cheese spread made with fresh cheese, herbs, shallots, vinegar, and olive oil.

It is often served as an appetizer with toast.

Recommended Restaurants: Try Cervelle de Canut at Le Bouchon des Filles or Les Lyonnais Bouchon, where it's a favorite dish.

Gratin Dauphinois: This creamy potato gratin,

cooked with thinly sliced

potatoes, cream, and garlic, is a soothing mainstay in the region's cuisine.

Recommended Restaurants: Try the Gratin Dauphinois at Le Sud or Brasserie Georges, both known for their substantial and wonderful versions of this dish.

Regional Specialties

Beaujolais Wine: Beaujolais wine, known for its light, fruity flavors, holds a unique position in the Rhone area and is celebrated annually during the Beaujolais Nouveau festival.

Recommended Wineries and Wine Bars: Visit Château de Pizay or Le Comptoir du Vin to sample and learn about Beaujolais wines.

Rosette de Lyon: This classic dry sausage from Lyon is produced with coarsely ground pork and seasoned with garlic and pepper for a rich and flavorful taste.

Recommended Charcuteries: Purchase Rosette de Lyon from a reputable charcuterie, such as Sibilia or Charcuterie Bobosse.

Coq au Vin: A classic French dish of chicken cooked in red wine, typically Beaujolais or Côtes du Rhône, with mushrooms, lardons, and onions.

Recommended Restaurants: Try Coq au Vin at La Mère Jean or La Traboule, where it is prepared using traditional techniques and ingredients.

Local Markets and Food Hall

Les Halles de Lyon Paul Bocuse: This famous food market, named after renowned chef Paul Bocuse, offers a vast selection of local produce, meats, cheeses, and gourmet products.

Must-try Stalls: Stop by Maison Sibilia for charcuterie and Fromagerie Mons for cheese, both popular sellers in Les Halles.

Visitor information: Open everyday from 7 a.m. to 10 p.m. Located at 102 Cours Lafayette, 69003 Lyon. Special events and tastings take place on a regular basis.

Other Notable Markets

Marché Saint-Antoine (Lyon): A bustling riverside market with fresh vegetables, local specialties, and handcrafted crafts.

Marché de la Croix-Rousse (Lyon): This market, known for its lively ambiance and broad assortment of food vendors, is popular with both locals and visitors.

Eating Experiences

Bouchons Lyonnais: Traditional Lyonnaise eateries with hearty, rustic meals and a friendly ambiance, offering a genuine eating experience.

Recommended Bouchons: For an authentic bouchon experience, visit Café Comptoir Abel, Chez Hugon, and Le Garet.

The Rhone area offers Michelin-starred restaurants with superb food and unique menus. Recommended Restaurants: For an exceptional dining experience, visit Restaurant Paul Bocuse, La Mère Brazier, or Têtedoie.

Casual Dining and Street Food: Experience local cuisine in a relaxing setting, with casual dining and street food selections.
Recommended Spots: For informal dining, go to Bistrot des Voraces, and for amazing street cuisine, visit Les Halles de Lyon's food trucks.

Cooking workshops and Culinary Tours
Cooking Classes: Hands-on cooking workshops provide a unique and immersive culinary experience, teaching traditional cuisine.
Recommended classes: Attend a cooking lesson at Plum Lyon Teaching Kitchen or In Cuisine for an educational and enjoyable experience.
Visitor Information: Class schedules and fees vary. Make an advance booking online.

Culinary Tours: Guided culinary tours provide insights into the region's food culture and samplings of local specialties.

Recommended Tours: Join tours with Lyon Food Tour or Original Food Tours for an entertaining and delicious adventure.

Visitor Information: Tour times and costs vary. Make an advance booking online.

Insider Tips and Recommendations: During the spring and autumn months, enjoy seasonal foods and local events. The Beaujolais Nouveau festival in November is a must-see for wine lovers.

For a one-of-a-kind eating experience, visit less well-known restaurants like Café du Peintre.

Visit smaller markets, such as Marché Monplaisir, for a more intimate and local experience.

When dining at a bouchon, expect communal seating and a relaxed atmosphere. Ask the staff for recommendations; they are generally delighted to share their favorite meals.

Renowned wineries and vineyards

The Rhone is one of France's leading wine-producing regions, known for its broad range of wines, including red, white, and rosé. The Rhone Valley has a winemaking tradition that dates back over 2,000 years and is known for its diverse terroirs, varietals, and appellations. The region is separated into Northern and Southern Rhone, with each having distinct wine styles and characteristics.

Wine Regions within Rhone

Northern Rhône: The Northern Rhône is renowned for its robust and complex Syrah-based red wines and aromatic Viognier-based whites. The region's steep, terraced vineyards benefit from a continental climate, which contributes to the wines' particular flavor profiles.

Key Appellations: Notable appellations include Côte-Rôtie, Hermitage, and Condrieu, which produce wines known for their quality and aging potential.

The Southern Rhône region is known for its red blends of Grenache, Syrah, and Mourvèdre, as well as aromatic and full-bodied white wines. The region has a Mediterranean climate with hot summers and mild winters, which is ideal for grape growing.

Key Appellations: Notable appellations include Châteauneuf-du-Pape, Gigondas, and Côtes du Rhône, which are noted for producing rich and expressive wines.

Recognized Wineries and Vineyards

Château de Beaucastel (Château-du-Pape): This historic estate (Chem. de Beaucastel , 84350 courthezon) is recognized for its coveted Châteauneuf-du-Pape wines, which are made from a blend of up to 13 grape varieties, resulting in complex and balanced wines.

Visitor Experience: Tours and tastings are available, which provide insight into the estate's history and winemaking process. Open Monday through Friday, 10 a.m. to 5:30 p.m. Tours cost €25 per person and should be booked in advance. Call +33 4 90 70 41 15

E. Guigal (Ampuis, Northern Rhône): Renowned for its Côte-Rôtie, Condrieu, and Hermitage wines, E. Guigal is a benchmark winery in the Northern Rhône, producing some of the region's greatest wines.

Visitor Experience: Visitors can take guided tours, try tastings, and visit the historic cellars.

Open Monday through Friday, 9 a.m. to 5 p.m. Tours cost €20 per person and should be booked in advance. Call +33 4 74 56 10 22

Domaine du Vieux Télégraphe (Châteauneuf-du-Pape): This renowned estate (3 Rte de Châteauneuf du page 84370 bedarrides), known for its powerful and exquisite Châteauneuf-du-Pape wines, offers a thorough dive into the region's terroir and winemaking traditions.

Visitor Experience: Tours and tastings include vineyard excursions and barrel samplings. Open Monday through Friday, 8:30 a.m. to 5:30 p.m. Call +33 4 90 33 00 31

Tours at Domaine Jean-Louis Chave (Mauves, Northern Rhône) cost €30 per person and require previous booking. The family-owned estate (11 Rue du traminer, 68420) is known for its Hermitage and Saint-Joseph wines, which showcase some of the best Syrah in the region.

Visitor Experience: Tours and tastings offer insight into the estate's winemaking process. Open Monday through Friday, 10 a.m. to 5 p.m. Tours cost €35 per person and should be booked in advance. Call +33 4 89 24 26 47

Wine Tasting Experiences

Tasting Rooms: Wine tasting experiences range from informal in-room tastings to more extensive, guided sessions that dig into the intricacies of each wine.

Recommended Tasting Rooms: For outstanding service and a diverse wine selection, visit Maison Chapoutier and Domaine Saint Préfert's tasting rooms.

Wine and Food Pairings: Some wineries provide wine and food pairing experiences, allowing visitors to sample local wines alongside regional specialties.

Recommended Experiences: Château La Nerthe

and Domaine de la Janasse offer wine and food pairings, with well-prepared dishes to complement the wines.

Wine Tours and Excursions

Guided Wine Tours: Experience the region's vineyards, cellars, and winemaking processes with knowledgeable guides.

Recommended Tour Operators: Booking with Rhône Wine Tours or Wine Safari Rhône. Tours are available every day, with fees beginning at €100 per person. Make an advance booking online.

Self-Guided Tours: Self-guided tours let you explore vineyards at your own speed, creating a more personalized experience.

Suggested Routes: Take recommended routes, such as the Côtes du Rhône wine route, and visit must-see wineries along the way. Use a map to organize your visits, taking into account opening hours and booking requirements.

Wine Festivals and Events

Annual Wine Events: Rhone wine festivals and events promote the local wine culture through tastings, excursions, and cultural activities.

Event Highlights: Immerse yourself in wine at the Fête des Vendanges in September or the Hermitage en Fête in June.

Visitor information: Check event dates, venues, and ticket purchasing choices online in advance.

Wine Education and Workshops

Wine Classes and Workshops: Learn about winemaking, tasting techniques, and pairings.

Recommended Workshops: Enroll in workshops at the Université du Vin in Suze-la-Rousse, which offers a variety of courses at all levels.

Classes are provided all year, with costs starting at €50 per session. Book online.

Insider Tips and Recommendations: For a more dynamic experience, visit during the growing season and harvest in spring or autumn.

For a truly unique experience, visit lesser-known wineries such as Domaine de la Vieille Julienne. Engage with local winemakers to receive personalized recommendations.

Etiquette and Tasting Tips: Sip and taste each wine while taking notes and asking questions. Do not hesitate to buy wines straight from the winery, and always appreciate the workers for their friendliness.

Food markets and culinary tours

The Rhone region is well-known for its bustling food market culture, which reflects the area's rich culinary heritage and dedication to fresh, local goods. These markets are an important part of everyday life, providing a variety of high-quality ingredients and unique culinary experiences that both locals and tourists enjoy.

Best Food Markets

Paul Bocuse (Lyon): Named after the legendary chef Paul Bocuse, this unique indoor food market is a gourmet paradise, showcasing a broad selection of high-quality products, including meats, cheeses, pastries, and seafood. Must-Visit merchants: Include must-see merchants like Maison Sibilia for charcuterie, Fromagerie Mons for cheeses, and Pignol for pastries. Visitor Information: Located at 102 Cours Lafayette in Lyon. Open Monday through Saturday from 7 a.m. to 7 p.m., and on Sunday from 9 a.m. Special events and tastings are frequently hosted on weekends.

Marché Saint-Antoine (Lyon): This popular riverside market is noted for its fresh fruit, baked products, flowers, and a range of local delicacies, providing a scenic shopping experience along the Saône River.

Must-Visit Vendors: Key vendors include local farmers offering seasonal fruits and vegetables, as well as artisan bakers and cheese sellers.

Visitor information: Located on Quai Saint-Antoine, Lyon. Open every day from 6 a.m. to 1 p.m., with the best selection accessible early in the morning.

Marché de la Croix-Rousse (Lyon): This busy market offers a broad assortment of food kiosks, including fresh vegetables and cooked delicacies.

Must-Visit Vendors: Notable vendors include local butchers, fishermen, and bakeries, which provide a wide range of delectable choices.

Visitor Information: Located on Boulevard de la Croix-Rousse, Lyon. The market is open every day from 6 a.m. to 1 p.m., with weekends being especially busy.

Other Notable Markets

Marché de Vienne: A historic market with local produce, meats, cheeses, and baked items, offering a cultural experience.

Marché de Valence: Known for its bright selection of fresh fruits, vegetables, and regional delicacies, this market is a must-see for foodies.

Market trips: trips explore local food markets and provide insights into vendors, goods, and food culture.

Recommended Market Tours: Les Halles de Lyon. Paul Bocuse and Marché Saint-Antoine provide guided tours that cover the market's history and highlight notable sellers.

Visitor Information: Tours depart many times every week, with fees beginning at €30 per person. Book ahead of time to ensure availability.

Culinary Workshops: Culinary workshops combine market trips and culinary classes to teach participants how to produce traditional dishes with fresh, local ingredients.

Recommended programs: Plum Lyon Teaching Kitchen and In Cuisine provide hands-on courses that combine market trips and cooking classes.

Visitor Information: Workshops are provided all week, with costs beginning at €100 per person. Check timetables and book in advance online.

Insider Tips and Recommendations

Best Times to Visit Markets: For the freshest produce and fewer crowds, go early in the morning. Weekdays are typically less busy than weekends.

Local Insights: For a more authentic experience, locals recommend visiting lesser-known marketplaces like Marché de la Croix-Rousse. Connect with sellers to discover hidden gems and local specialties.

Shopping Tip: Bring reusable bags and small coins for purchases, and be ready to try products. Ask merchants for recommendations and culinary tips.

Extra Experiences

Special Market Events: Many markets feature special events or festivals, such as seasonal fairs, Christmas markets, or food festivals, providing unique gastronomic experiences.

Visitor Information: Check market websites or local tourist information for event dates, locations, and what to expect.

Food Tasting Experiences: In markets or on culinary tours, sample local specialties such as cheeses, charcuterie, pastries, and wines.

Recommended Experiences: Participate in tastings at Les Halles de Lyon Paul Bocuse, or go on a culinary tour with several tasting stops.

Visitor Information: Tasting sessions are

frequently included in market trips or can be scheduled independently. Prices and schedules vary, so check online for more information and book in advance.

Chapter Four

Shopping

Local Crafts and Souvenirs

The Rhone region is rich in cultural heritage and artisanal traditions, as well as a wide range of local products and souvenirs. Visitors can find one-of-a-kind things that reflect the region's history and craftsmanship, including homemade delicacies, artisanal fabrics, pottery, and silk products.

Les Halles de Lyon is a top market for local crafts and souvenirs.

Paul Bocuse (Lyon): This legendary indoor food market offers homemade dishes, specialty items, and unusual souvenirs.

Must-See Vendors include Maison Sibilia for charcuterie, Voisin for chocolates, and Les

Miels de Joyeuse for honey.

Visitor Information: Located at 102 Cours Lafayette in Lyon. Open Monday through Saturday from 7 a.m. to 7 p.m., and on Sunday from 9 a.m. Arrive early to avoid crowds and ensure the finest selection.

Marché de la Création (Lyon): An open-air market for local artists and craftsmen selling handmade jewelry, pottery, paintings, and other art objects.

Must-See Stalls: Look for unusual pottery, bespoke jewelry, and original artworks by local artists.

Visitor Information: Located at Quai Romain Rolland in Lyon. Open every Sunday from 8 a.m. to 1 p.m. For the best variety, visit in the morning.

Marché Provençal (Valence): This market specializes in Provençal crafts, like lavender goods, olive wood carvings, and traditional fabrics.

Must-See Stalls: Look for merchants selling original regional crafts and gifts.

Visitor Information: Located in Place de la République in Valence. Open Tuesday, Thursday, and Saturday from 7 a.m. to 1 p.m. The best time to visit is in the morning.

Special Stores for Local Crafts and Souvenirs

Boutique de Musées (Lyon): A museum shop offering art-inspired souvenirs, including prints, sculptures, and museum-themed items.

Must-Buy Items: replicas of well-known artworks, museum catalogs, and special products.

Visitor Information: The Musée des Beaux-Arts is located at 20 Place des Terreaux in Lyon. Open daily, except Tuesday, from 10 a.m. to 6 p.m.

La Maison des Canuts (Lyon): This store celebrates Lyon's silk-weaving legacy and sells scarves, ties, and home decor items.

Must-Buy Items: Handcrafted silk scarves, ties, and accessories. Look for opportunities to provide demonstrations or hold workshops.

Visitor Information: Located at 10-12 Rue d'Ivry in Lyon. Open Tuesday through Saturday from 10 a.m. to 6:30 p.m.

Atelier de Soierie (Lyon): A workshop and boutique that showcases classic silk-screening processes and offers hand-painted silk goods.

Must-Buys: Hand-painted scarves, ties, and ornamental panels.

Visitor Information: Located at 33 Rue Romarin in Lyon. Open Monday through Saturday from 10 a.m. to 6 p.m. Guided tours are available upon request.

L'Atelier de Lutherie (Valence): Specializes in handmade musical instruments, especially string instruments created by local musicians.

Must-Buy Items: Handcrafted instruments and accessories available for special orders or repairs.

Visitor information: Located at 15 Rue des Alpes in Valence. Open Monday through Friday from 9 a.m. to 6 p.m.

Unique Local Products

Regional Food Products: Rhône wines, artisanal cheeses, cured meats, and honey are excellent mementos.

Recommended Purchases: wines from well-known wineries, cheeses from local dairy farms, and honey from regional beekeepers.

Visitor Information: Tips for buying and transporting food items as keepsakes.

Handmade Pottery and Ceramics: Traditional ceramics from the Rhone area, highlighting craftsmanship and cultural relevance.

Recommended Shops: local pottery studios and artisan marketplaces.

Visitor Information: How to select and pack pottery and ceramics for safe transit.

Traditional textiles and fabrics, including Provençal, embroidered linens, and silk goods.

Recommended shops: specialty fabric stores and artisan businesses.

Visitor Information: Tips for buying and shipping textiles.

Insider Tips and Recommendations

Bargaining and Shopping Etiquette: While bargaining is not common in France, courteous negotiation is permitted in marketplaces. Always greet sellers with a friendly "bonjour" and show appreciation for their craftsmanship.

Best Time to Shop: Visit markets early in the morning to get the finest choices and avoid crowds. Weekdays are typically less busy than weekends.

Local insights: For unique finds, locals recommend checking out lesser-known marketplaces and stores. Engage with artists to learn about their skills and uncover hidden gems.

Additional Experiences

Craft Workshops and Demonstrations: Tourists can participate in craft workshops or observe demonstrations by local artisans.

Recommended Workshops: Workshops or demos offered by local artists or cultural centers, such as silk painting at Atelier de Soierie or pottery classes at nearby studios.

Visitor Information: Specifics, such as schedules, costs, and how to book these activities.

Fashion Boutiques and Designer Stores

The Rhone region has a vibrant fashion culture that combines traditional and contemporary designs. Local designers and international brands are widely represented, giving fashion fans a diverse shopping experience.

Top Fashion Boutiques

Lyon: Lyon is a fashion hub with boutiques featuring local and international designers.

Le Village des Créateurs: A communal area for rising designers to present their current collections, offering unique and inventive fashion pieces.

Visitor Information: Located in Passage Thiaffait in Lyon. Open Monday through Saturday from 10 a.m. to 7 p.m. Notable designers include Constance L, Lucien, and Beliza.

Antoine et Lili offers a vibrant and diverse combination of apparel, accessories, and home design.

Visitor Information: Located at 5 Quai Sarrail in Lyon. Open Monday through Saturday from 10:30 a.m. to 7:30 p.m. Popular goods include colorful outfits and unusual accessories.

Chez Laurette: A shop that specializes in vintage-inspired fashion with a carefully curated assortment of apparel and accessories.

Visitor Information: Located at 17 Rue de Brest in Lyon. Open Tuesday through Saturday from 11 a.m. to 7 p.m. Retro outfits and distinctive accessories are popular items.

Valence: Valence is an emerging fashion shopping destination with boutiques and designer retailers.

La Petite Boutique: Description: Known for exquisite and contemporary fashion, showcasing pieces from both local and international designers.

Visitor Information: Located at 23 Grande Rue in Valence. Open Monday through Saturday from 10 a.m. to 6 p.m. Chic clothes and fashionable accessories are among the top sellers.

L'Atelier de Valence: Provides a combination of modern and vintage fashion, emphasizing distinctive and sustainable pieces.

Visitor Information: Located at 12 Rue des Alpes in Valence. Open Tuesday through Saturday from 10 a.m. to 6 p.m. Popular goods include sustainable clothes and vintage treasures.

Top Designer Stores

Lyon: Lyon is a fashion-forward city with a range of designer stores featuring established and new designers.

Hermès: Description: An iconic French luxury brand known for its high-end couture, accessories, and leather products. Visitor Information: Located at 52 Rue du Président Édouard Herriot in Lyon. Open Monday through Saturday from 10 a.m. to 6:30 p.m. Popular goods include silk scarves and leather bags.

Louis Vuitton is a prominent fashion brand that offers luxury products such as apparel, accessories, and luggage. Visitor Information: Located at 70 Rue du Président Édouard Herriot in Lyon. Open Monday through Saturday from 10 a.m. to 7 p.m. Monogrammed bags and exquisite clothes are popular commodities.

Chanel: Recognized for its timeless elegance and refined designs. Visitor Information: Located at 71 Rue du

Président Édouard Herriot in Lyon. Open Monday through Saturday from 10 a.m. to 6:30 p.m. Popular goods include traditional tweed coats and signature scents.

Valence's designer stores sell high-end fashion and luxury items.

Christian Dior Boutique: Description: Offers high-end apparel and accessories.

Visitor information: Located at 11 Rue de l'Université in Valence. Open Monday through Saturday from 10 a.m. to 6 p.m. Elegant outfits and couture pieces are very popular.

Shopping Districts and Malls

La Part-Dieu (Lyon): A large shopping center with fashion shops, designer stores, and global brands.

Visitor Information: Located at 17 Rue du Docteur Bouchut in Lyon. Open Monday through Saturday from 9:30 a.m. to 8 p.m. Zara,

H&M, and Printemps are all well-known stores.

Confluence (Lyon) is a modern shopping and entertainment complex with a mix of high-end and mid-range fashion stores.

Visitor Information: Located at 112 Cours Charlemagne in Lyon. Open Monday through Saturday from 10 a.m. to 8 p.m. The Kooples, Maje, and Sephora are among the most well-known stores.

Centre Commercial Victor Hugo (Valence): A popular shopping destination for fashion boutiques and designer businesses.

Visitor Information: Address: 9 Avenue Victor Hugo, Valence. Open Monday through Saturday from 10 a.m. to 7 p.m. Notable retailers include Mango and Sandro.

Unique Shopping Experiences

Fashion Shows and Events: Visit notable fashion shows, events, or pop-up stores to discover new designers and trends.

Visitor Information: Event dates, locations, and directions to attend. For example, Lyon Fashion Week takes place in October.

Personal Shopping Services: Personalized shopping experiences with expert guidance.

Recommended Services: Maison de Mode in Lyon offers personalized shopping. Reservations can be made online or by phoning ahead.

Sustainable and Ethical Fashion: Highlight the growing trend of sustainable and ethical fashion boutiques that provide eco-friendly and socially responsible products.

Recommended boutiques: Mention boutiques

like Joya in Lyon, which is known for its ecological fashion items.

Insider Tips and Recommendations

Shopping Etiquette: Greet personnel with "Bonjour" and respect the merchandise. In high-end boutiques, it is common to let the staff walk you through the inventory.

The Best Times to Shop: Avoid crowds by going early in the morning or late afternoon. Weekdays are typically less busy than weekends.

Local insights: Locals recommend visiting hidden treasures, such as Rue Auguste Comte in Lyon, to find unusual boutiques and lesser-known designer outlets.

Antiques and Collectibles

The Rhone region has a rich history and a wide selection of antiques and antiquities. Visitors can discover a wide range of objects reflecting the area's cultural and historical legacy, including antique furniture and artwork, as well as vintage jewelry and rare books.

Top Antique Markets

Les Puces du Canal (Lyon): This renowned flea market offers a wide range of antiques and vintage products, including furniture, decor, apparel, and accessories.

Must-Visit Stalls: Keep an eye out for vendors such as Brocanteur des Puces for antique furniture and Bijoux Vintage for beautiful vintage jewelry.

Location: 3 Rue Eugène Pottier, Villeurbanne.

Open Thursday, Saturday, and Sunday from 7

a.m. to 1 p.m. It's best to go early for the best finds.

Marché aux Puces de Villeurbanne (Lyon): A popular flea market with a variety of antiques, collectibles, and second-hand goods.

Must-Visit Stalls: Popular merchants include Antiques et Objets for eclectic antiques and La Malle Ancienne for vintage baggage.

It is located at 3 Avenue des Canuts in Villeurbanne. Open Saturday and Sunday from 6 a.m. to 2 p.m. Arrive early to avoid the throng.

Marché de la Création (Lyon): An open-air market with local artists and craftsmen selling unique handmade products, vintage pieces, and collectibles.

Must-See Stalls: Popular vendors include Art et Artisanat for handmade crafts and Vintage Chic for retro items.

Visitor Information: Located on Quai Romain Rolland, Lyon. Open Sundays from 8 a.m. to 1 p.m. For a more relaxing experience, arrive in the morning.

Top Antique Businesses

Lyon: Lyon is a hub for antique enthusiasts, with a variety of businesses providing historical and collectible things.

Galerie Antiquités Lyon: Description: Renowned for its wide collection of high-quality antiques, including furniture, artwork, and decorative items.

Visitor Information: Located at 10 Rue Auguste Comte in Lyon. Open Monday through Saturday from 10 a.m. to 6 p.m. Popular pieces include Louis XV furniture and Baroque art.

Antiquités Rive Gauche: This store curates a collection of antiques and vintage objects, with a concentration on French and European products.

Visitor Information: Located at 5 Quai de la Pêcherie in Lyon. Open Tuesday through Saturday from 11 a.m. to 6 p.m. Popular items include old clocks and European porcelain.

Atelier des Antiquaires is known for its diversified collection of antiquities, such as rare books, old jewelry, and historical relics.

Visitor Information: Located at 18 Rue Auguste Comte in Lyon. Open Tuesday through Saturday from 10 a.m. to 6 p.m. Antique brooches and rare first edition books are popular products.

Valence: Valence's growing antiques industry includes stores selling collectibles and vintage items.

Antiquités Valence: Specializes in antiques and collectibles, such as furniture, artwork, and decorative goods.

Visitor Information: Located at 45 Rue Madier de Montjau in Valence. Open Monday through Saturday from 10 a.m. to 6 p.m. Popular pieces include Impressionist paintings and Art Deco furniture.

La Brocante de Valence: Offers a combination of antiques and vintage things, with a concentration on rare and difficult-to-find artifacts.
Visitor Information: Located at 12 Rue Perrot de Verdun in Valence. Open Tuesday through Saturday from 11 a.m. to 6 p.m. Popular things include old postcards and antique lights.

Unique Shopping Experiences
Antique Fairs and Events: The Rhone area hosts notable antique fairs and events where visitors can find unique and uncommon things.
Visitor Information: One example is the Lyon Antiques Fair, which takes place every April.

Check your local event listings for timetables and locations.

Antique Auctions: Attend antique auctions and bid on rare and valuable objects.

Visitor Information: The Hôtel des Ventes de Lyon, a reputable auction house, holds auctions on a monthly basis. Check their website for timetables and participation information.

Insider Tips and Recommendations

Bargaining and Shopping Etiquette: Be polite and respectful. Negotiating prices is appropriate in markets, but less so in established antique businesses. Begin with a friendly "Bonjour" and ask if a discount is available.

Best Times to Shop: Early mornings, especially on weekends, are perfect for exploring markets and finding the best assortment. Weekdays are generally quieter for store visits.

Local Insights: Locals recommend visiting

Lyon's Rue Auguste Comte for its concentration of antique shops and hidden jewels.

Additional Experiences

Antique Restoration Services: In the Rhone region, antique restoration services allow travelers to restore and preserve their purchases. Recommended Services: The Lyon-based Atelier de Restauration specializes in furniture restoration. Bookings can be made online or over the phone.

Antique Workshops and Tours: Tourists can participate in workshops or guided tours of antiques and collectibles.

Visitor Information: Workshops are frequently offered by local artisans, such as those at Atelier des Antiquaires. Check timetables and prices online, and make reservations in advance.

Chapter Five

Accommodation

Luxury Hotels

The Rhone region's premium hotels combine historical elegance with modern amenities. Visitors may anticipate high-end accommodations with outstanding service, delicious dining, and one-of-a-kind experiences in both bustling cities and picturesque countryside settings.

The list of top luxury hotels in major cities includes:

Hotel Le Royal Lyon. This 5-star hotel is noted for its gorgeous decor, great service, and prime position in the center of Lyon.

Amenities: Gourmet dining at the on-site restaurant, fitness center, spa services, luxury rooms, and free WiFi.

Visitor Information: Located at 20 Place Bellecour 69002, Lyon. Contact us at +33 4 78 37 57 31. Prices range from €250 to €600 per night.

Villa Florentine: A magnificent hotel set in a former convent with stunning views of Lyon and the surrounding area.

Amenities include a panoramic pool, gourmet restaurant, wellness center, historic architecture, and luxury accommodations with modern amenities.

Visitor Information: Located at 25 Montée Saint-Barthélémy, 69005 in Lyon. Contact them at +33 4 72 56 56 56. Prices range from €300 to €700 per night.

Cour des Loges: This premium hotel in the historic Old Town blends Renaissance architecture with modern amenities.
Features: fine dining, spa, rooftop patio, luxury rooms and suites, and personalized service.

Visitor Information: Located at 6 Rue du Boeuf in Lyon. Contact us at +33 4 72 77 44 44. The price range is €280-€650 per night.

Valence

Maison Pic: Prestigious luxury hotel with Michelin-starred restaurant and great service.

Amenities include gourmet dining, beautiful accommodations, a garden, personalized service, and a cooking school.

Visitor Information: Located at 285 Avenue Victor Hugo, 26000 in Valence.

Contact us at +33 4 75 44 15 32. Prices range from €350 to €900 per night.

Hotel France: An elegant hotel with excellent accommodations and a central location in Valence.

Amenities: Gourmet restaurant, contemporary rooms, bar, concierge services, and complimentary Wi-Fi.

Visitor

Information: Located at 16 Boulevard du Général de Gaulle in Valence. Contact them at +33 4 75 43 00 87. Prices range from €200 to €500 per night.

Luxury Hotels in Scenic Locations Chateau de Bagnols: This luxury hotel, housed in a medieval castle, provides a unique and historic lodging experience.

Amenities include fine restaurants, a spa, stunning gardens, luxury apartments with period furniture, and castle excursions.

Visitor Info: Located in 118 Pl. de la mairie, 69620 Bagnols. Contact us at +33 4 74 71 40 00. The price range is €400-€1200 each night.

Domaine de Clairefontaine: A luxurious estate

with peaceful settings, outstanding service, and elegant accommodations.

Amenities: Gourmet restaurant, lovely grounds, swimming pool, spacious rooms, and event spaces for weddings and conferences.

Visitor Information: Located at 105 Chemin des Fontanettes in Chonas-l'Amballan. Contact us at +33 4 74 58 81 52. Prices range from €250 to €600 per night.

Boutique Hotels and Bed & Breakfasts

The Rhone region has a charming selection of boutique hotels and bed and breakfasts, each offering customized service, distinctive decor, and intimate surroundings. These lodgings combine historical charm with modern amenities, providing guests with unforgettable experiences.

Top Boutique Hotels in Major Cities Lyon

Hotel des Artistes: A beautiful boutique hotel  with an artistic theme, situated along the Saône River and allowing quick access to Lyon's cultural sites. Amenities: Individually designed rooms, a comfortable lounge, personalized service, free Wi-Fi, and breakfast selections.

Visitor Information Located at 8 Rue Gaspard André, Pl. des Célestins, 69002. Contact us at +33 4 78 42 04 88. The price range is €100-€250 per night.

Mama Shelter Lyon: A stylish boutique hotel with

contemporary decor and an energetic atmosphere, ideal for modern tourists.

Amenities: rooftop bar, modern rooms with smart TVs, common areas, an on-site restaurant, and complimentary Wi-Fi.

Visitor Information: Located at 13 Rue Domer,

69007, Lyon. Contact them at +33 4 78 02 58 00. Prices range from €90 to €200 each night.

Valence

Hotel de la Villeon: A beautiful boutique hotel in a historic building, offering a blend of classic charm and modern conveniences.

Amenities include stylish accommodations, a garden, gourmet breakfast, and free Wi-Fi.

Visitor Information: Address: 2 Rue Davity, 07300 Tournon-sur-Rhône. Contact us at +33 4 75 06 97 50. The price range is €150-€350 per night.

Charming Bed & Breakfasts

La Bicyclette Fleurie (Villefranche-sur-Saône):

A charming bed & breakfast giving a warm and friendly atmosphere in a picturesque village setting. Amenities include comfortable rooms, delicious breakfast, bicycle rentals, and garden access.

Visitor Information: Located at 2 chemin de traverse, 38460 villemoirieu. Contact us at +33 4 74 90 06 55. The price range is €80-€150 per night.

Le Clos Saint Paul (Vienne): A magnificent bed and breakfast in a historic mansion, offering personalized service and gorgeous surroundings.

Amenities include stylish rooms, a garden, a delicious breakfast, and

complimentary Wi-Fi.

Visitor Information: Located at 71 Chem de la rouguiere, 06480. Contact them at +33 4 93 32 56 81d. Prices range from €100 to €200 per night.

Le Jardin de Beauvoir (Lyon): A beautiful bed & breakfast in the center of Lyon, offering a calm getaway with gardens and pleasant rooms. Amenities include homemade breakfast, garden views, individual service, and free Wi-Fi.

Visitor Information: Address: 8 Rue de Trion, 69005 Lyon. Contact them at +33 6 03 67 27 84.

The price range is €120-€250 per night.

Budget-Friendly Accommodations

The Rhone region provides a varied choice of low-cost hotels that are both comfortable and convenient. Travelers can find cost-effective solutions for exploring the region.

Top Budget Hotels in Major Cities

Lyon

Hôtel Berlioz: This budget-friendly hotel is noted for its central

location and comfortable rooms, making it a convenient base to explore Lyon.

Amenities include free Wi-Fi, a 24-hour front desk, and modest breakfast selections.

Visitor Information: Located at 12 Cours Charlemagne, 69002 in Lyon. Contact us at +33 4 78 42 30 31. The price range is €60-€120 per night.

Ibis Lyon Part Dieu Les Halles: This budget hotel provides modern accommodations and close access to public transit, making it ideal for budget-conscious tourists. Amenities include free Wi-Fi, air conditioning, a bar, and an on-site restaurant.

Visitor Information: Located at 78 Rue de Bonnel, 69003 Lyon. Contact us at +33 4 78 62 98 89. The price range is €70-€130 per night.

Meininger Hotel Lyon Centre Berthelot: This hotel is popular among budget-conscious travelers due to its lively environment and handy location.

Amenities include a communal kitchen, free Wi-Fi, family rooms, and a living area.

Visitor Information: Located at 7 Rue Professeur

Zimmermann, 69007 in Lyon. Contact us at +33 4 81 65 15 00. The price range is €50-€110 per night.

Valence

Hotel Les Negociants: Located in the heart of Valence, this cheap hotel provides pleasant

accommodations and courteous service.

Amenities include free Wi-Fi, a restaurant, and breakfast options.

Visitor Information: Located at 27 Avenue Pierre Semard, 26000 in Valence. Contact us at +33 4 75 44 01 86. Prices range from €60 to €100 per night.

Apartment City Value Center: This affordable  aparthotel provides fully equipped flats, making it perfect for extended visits.

Amenities include kitchen facilities, free Wi-Fi, and parking.

Visitor Information: Located at 6 Rue Poncet in Valence. Contact us at +33 4 56 58 97 97. Prices range from €50 to €90 per night.

Hostels and Guesthouses

Alter's Hostel (Lyon): This eco-friendly hostel

 provides affordable lodgings and a

community-focused ambiance.

Amenities include shared dormitories, a common kitchen, free Wi-Fi, and scheduled activities.

Visitor Information: Located at 32 Quai Arloing, 69009 in Lyon. Contact us at +33 4 26 18 05 28. Prices range from €20 to €50 per night.

SLO Living Hostel (Lyon): A modern hostel that provides economical lodging and a friendly setting, ideal for meeting fellow travelers.

Amenities include private and shared rooms, a bar, free Wi-Fi, and a shared lounge.

Visitor Information: Located at 5 Rue Bonnefoi, 69003 in Lyon. Contact us at +33 4 78 59 06 90. Prices range from €25 to €60 per night.

Le Clos de la Glycine (Avignon): This delightful guesthouse offers budget-friendly accommodations in a historical setting, delivering a comfortable and quaint experience. Amenities include free Wi-Fi, breakfast selections, and a garden.
Visitor Information: Located at 38 place de la

poste, 84220 in Roussillon. Contact us at +33 4 90 05 60 13. The price range is €60-€120.

Unique Accommodations

The Rhone region is home to a number of one-of-a-kind accommodations. These lodgings, ranging from vineyard estates surrounded by rolling hills to beautiful farmhouses secluded in the countryside, provide an immersive and unforgettable experience that highlights the region's natural beauty and historical legacy.

Top Vineyard Stays

Château de la Chaize (Beaujolais): This charming vineyard estate offers elegant lodgings amidst beautiful vines and historic architecture.

Amenities include wine tastings, guided vineyard tours, nicely appointed accommodations, excellent cuisine, and a scenic setting.

Visitor Information: Located at 500 roue de la chaize - 69460 Odenas. Contact them at +33 4 74 03 41 05. Prices range from €150 to €300 per night.

Domaine des Vignes (Saint-Joseph): This vineyard stay is known for its stunning setting, superb wines, and cozy and inviting atmosphere.

Amenities: wine cellar tours, picnic spots, pleasant lodging, and a welcoming, family-run environment.

Visitor Information: Located at 07300 Mauves in Saint-Joseph. Contact them at +33 4 75 08 30 32. The price range is €120-€250 per night.

Le Clos de la Bastide (Côtes du Rhône): This lovely vineyard stay offers breathtaking vistas and a peaceful hideaway, making it an excellent choice for wine connoisseurs.

Amenities include wine tastings, vineyard walks, comfy accommodations, cooked breakfasts, and peaceful settings. Visitor Information: Located in 84110 Vaison-la-Romaine, Côtes du Rhône. Contact them at +33 4 90 36 02 16. The price range is €130-€280 per night.

Charming Farmhouses

Mas de l'Olivier (Drôme Provençale): This rustic farmhouse provides a genuine rural experience and is ideal for nature enthusiasts.

Amenities include farm-to-table meals, large rooms, a swimming pool, and the opportunity to engage with farm animals. Visitor Information: Located in 26170 Buis-les-Baronnies in Drôme Provençale.

Contact us at +33 4 66 89 06 40. Prices range from €100 to €200 per night.

Ferme de la Huppe (Vaucluse): A historic farmhouse that offers a calm and delightful escape with

tastefully appointed rooms and gorgeous surroundings.

Amenities: Traditional Provençal cuisine, gardens, bike trails, and a relaxing atmosphere.

Visitor Information: Located at Hameau des Pourquiers, 570 route de goult RD 156, 84220 Gordes in Vaucluse. Contact us at +33 4 90 72 12 25. The price range is €120-€220 per night.

Domaine des Escaunes (Gard): This magnificent farmhouse combines traditional charm with modern comfort and is nestled in a picturesque location.

Amenities: wine tasting, gourmet dining, opulent

accommodations, a pool, and stunning gardens.

Visitor Information: Situated at 5 Rue des bourgades, 30210 Sernhac. Contact us at +33 4 66 37 49 44. Prices range from €150 to €300 per night.

Booking Tips and Advice

1. Peak Seasons and Reservations: Book early for busy seasons (spring and summer), and hunt for special bargains or packages during the off-season.

2. Reputable internet booking platforms for luxury hotels in the Rhone region include Booking.com, Expedia, and hotel websites.

3. Cancellation Policies: Understanding hotels' cancellation policies and the value of flexible booking alternatives.

Check cancellation policies before booking, and choose flexible choices whenever possible.

4. Special Amenities and Services

Spa and Wellness: hotels offer top-notch facilities featuring;

- Massage and body treatments
- Skin care and beauty treatments
- Saunas, stream rooms, and pools
- Fitness centers

Eating Experiences: Enjoy gourmet dining at Michelin-starred restaurants and exclusive culinary experiences with:

Fine dining menus

- Wine tastings and pairings
- Seasonal and local ingredients

Unique Features: Take advantage of features such as private cinemas, exclusive event access, personalized butler services, curated art collections, and private gardens or rooftop terraces.

Chapter Six

Transportation

Public Transportation

The Rhone region has an extensive public transit system, making it simple to tour its cities and scenery. Trains, buses, and trams are reliable and widespread, connecting major cities such as Lyon, Valence, and Avignon to smaller towns and attractions. Public transportation is efficient, economical, and often a handy method to get around the area.

Train Travel

Main Train Routes and Stations: The Rhone area has a well-developed train network. Key roadways connect Lyon, Valence, Avignon, and other key cities. The region is also connected to other sections of France, including Paris and

Marseille.

Key Stations: Lyon Part-Dieu, Lyon Perrache, and Valence TGV are key hubs for both local and long-distance trains.

Schedules and Frequency: Trains run on a regular basis, with current schedules available both online and at stations.

Regional and High-Speed Trains: Regional (TER) trains serve local routes, connecting smaller towns and rural areas. High-speed (TGV) trains connect the region with other major French cities, allowing for faster travel times.

Ticketing and Booking: Tickets can be purchased online, at ticket machines, or at station counters. Advance booking is recommended, particularly for high-speed trains.

Passes and Discounts: For limitless travel, consider a rail pass, such as the France Rail

Pass, or look into discounts for visitors, students, and retirees.

Additional Tips: Validate your ticket before boarding. Arrive early, especially on TGV trains, to take advantage of amenities such as luggage storage and on-board Wi-Fi.

Bus Travel

Local and Intercity Buses: The Rhone region's bus network offers both local services within cities and intercity routes linking different sections of the region. Buses are a convenient way to reach locations not served by railroads.

Key Operators: Major operators include TCL (Transports en Commun Lyonnais) in Lyon, as well as Ouibus and FlixBus for further distances.

Timetables and Booking: Schedules are available online and at bus stations. Tickets can frequently be purchased on board or online.

Practical Tip: Some local buses need precise

change, so bring coins. Keep track of the last bus times, and consider using transit applications for real-time schedules and route planning.

Car Rental and Driving Tips

Major Car Rental Companies: Avis, Hertz, Europcar, and local providers offer a variety of automobiles throughout the Rhone area.

Rental places: Airports (such as Lyon-Saint-Exupéry), train stations, and city centers are popular rental destinations.

Booking and pricing: It is recommended that you book ahead of time, compare prices, and double-check the rental agreement for inclusions such as insurance and mileage allowances.

Road Conditions and Signage: The Rhone region's roadways are well-maintained and have clear signage. Motorways (autoroutes) are quick and efficient, while regional roads provide scenic paths.

Toll Roads: Be ready for toll roads (péages). Payment can be made with cash or credit card, and the fee varies according to the distance traveled.

In cities and towns, parking options include public spaces and streets. Parking laws and costs vary, so check signs for specifics.

Cost and Restrictions: In city centers, expect to pay for parking. Use parking applications to identify open spaces and check for limitations, such as time limits.

Driving Etiquette and Rules: Follow speed limits, use seatbelts, and be familiar with French road signs. Roundabouts are ubiquitous, and vehicles already in them have the right of way.

Important Considerations: An International Driving Permit (IDP) may be necessary. Be familiar with local driving customs and traffic rules.

Alternative Transportation Options
Bicycles and Bike Rentals
Major cities like Lyon provide bike rentals and bike-sharing systems, such as Vélo'v. Cycling is an excellent method to see both metropolitan areas and scenic paths along the Rhône River.

Taxis and Ride-Sharing: Description: Taxis are common in most cities and towns. Ride-sharing services such as Uber are also available in the region, giving handy transit options.

Navigating the Region: Use GPS or navigation apps to plan routes when driving or taking public transportation. These apps help you avoid traffic and identify the shortest routes.

Safety Tip: Be cautious in remote regions, keep valuables safe, and keep an eye out for pickpockets, especially in crowded areas.

Routes for cycling and walking

The Rhone Valley is a biker's and walker's dream, with a rich tapestry of stunning landscapes, historical landmarks, and cultural experiences. Whether touring the beautiful vineyards, rolling countryside, or picturesque villages, these activities offer an intimate and immersive view of the region.

Popular bicycle routes include the Via Rhône, which follows the Rhône River from Lake Geneva to the Mediterranean Sea. It's popular with cyclists of all skill levels, with a combination of flat and mountainous terrain.

Key Sections: The Rhone region's key segments are Lyon to Vienne, recognized for its metropolitan landscapes and old architecture, and Valence to Montélimar, which goes through scenic countryside and lovely villages.

Difficulties and Scenery: The route ranges from simple to moderate difficulties, with riders taking in riverbank views, vineyards, and historic landmarks along the way.

Practical Tips: Cyclists should rent bikes locally, carry maps, and follow safety precautions, such as wearing helmets. It is also important to bring water and snacks, particularly in rural places.

Beaujolais Wine Route: A lovely cycling route through the Beaujolais wine region, known for its undulating vineyards and attractive villages. It's a voyage through one of France's most renowned wine regions.

Points of Interest: Wineries and tasting facilities offer bikers the opportunity to try local wines. The path also includes historical landmarks and stunning views.

Best Time to Visit: This route is best cycled during the wine harvest season, which runs from late summer to early fall, when the vineyards are at their most vibrant.

Practical Tips: Bike rentals are available, and guided excursions can enrich the experience by providing information about the region's viticulture and history. Accommodations range from cozy bed and breakfasts to lavish mansions.

Notable Walking Trails

Pilgrimage Route to Santiago de Compostela (GR65): The GR65 is a portion of the famed Camino de Santiago pilgrimage route, giving a spiritual and cultural trip across the Rhone area.

Key Segments: The track from Lyon to Le Puy-en-Velay is especially noteworthy, traveling through historic towns, tranquil scenery, and prominent religious sites.

Trail Conditions: The trail varies in difficulty, with well-marked paths and amenities like rest breaks and lodging accessible along the way.

Practical Tips: Walkers should bring essentials such as strong shoes, water, and protective gear.

Respect for local customs and traditions is essential because the road is a vital pilgrimage trail.

Monts d'Ardèche Regional Nature Park: This nature park provides walking trails through varied environments such as mountains, forests, and rivers. It's a sanctuary for nature lovers and outdoorsmen.

Highlight Trails: Notable trails include the "Volcanic Hike," which explores old volcanic formations, and the "Canyons and Castles Walk," which features breathtaking landscape and historical monuments.

Flora and Fauna: The park is home to a diverse range of plants and animals, including uncommon species. Hikers can enjoy seeing local fauna and geological highlights.

Practical Tip: Spring and autumn are the greatest times to visit because the weather is warm. Wearing suitable gear and staying on defined routes are two important safety precautions.

Resources for Cycling and Walking

Maps and Guides: Available at tourist offices, bookstores, and online. These tools provide critical information on route difficulty, distance, and areas of interest.

Equipment and Rentals: Bike and gear rentals are available in large cities such as Lyon and Valence, with alternatives to suit all abilities of bikers. Walking equipment can be leased or purchased locally.

Guided Tours and Apps: Guided tours provide expert knowledge and a more structured experience, whereas apps provide navigation aids and information on local sights.

River Cruises

River cruises on the Rhône River provide a unique approach to experiencing the Rhone area, combining relaxation with the opportunity to see cultural landmarks and magnificent scenery. These cruises are popular due to their relaxed pace and lavish amenities.

Popular River Cruise Routes

Lyon to Avignon: This popular route takes passengers through some of the Rhone region's most attractive and culturally rich places, including historic towns and famous wine districts.

Key Destinations: Notable destinations include Tournon-sur-Rhône, known for its medieval castle; Viviers, a lovely riverbank town; and Avignon, known for the Palais des Papes.

Duration and Itinerary: Cruises are typically 7-10 days long, with daily excursions to local attractions and cultural experiences.

Onboard Amenities: Ships frequently offer excellent cuisine, entertainment, and guided excursions, resulting in a premium vacation experience.

The Burgundy and Provence Route blends Burgundy's culinary delights and historical attractions with the scenic beauty and cultural richness of Provence.

Key Stops: Visit Chalon-sur-Saône, noted for its wine; Mâcon, a city with a rich Romanesque past; and Arles, famous for its Roman remains.

Unique Experiences: Cruises may include wine tastings, excursions to Roman sites, and culinary tours, providing a deeper understanding of the region's culture.

To choose a river cruise, consider reputable operators such as Viking River Cruises, AmaWaterways, and Uniworld, which provide diverse itineraries and experiences.

Package Options: Choose from short vacations

to specialized cruises like wine tours, as well as all-inclusive packages that include meals, activities, and onboard amenities.

Booking Tip

Book early to get the greatest rates and cabin options. When making a reservation, keep the type of cabin, itinerary preferences, and pricing package in mind.

Accessibility and Suitability: Many cruises cater to those with mobility challenges, including options for families, elders, and solitary travelers.

Chapter Seven

Day Trip and Excursion

Charming Villages and Towns

The Rhone valley is filled with lovely villages and towns, each with their own unique blend of history, architecture, and natural beauty. These destinations offer an insight into the region's rich cultural heritage and traditions, making them perfect for day trips and excursions.

The Palais des Papes, which served as the Pope's home in the 14th century. It is a UNESCO World Heritage Site and one of Europe's largest and most significant medieval Gothic constructions. Visitors can tour the magnificent halls, chapels, and private rooms.

Pont d'Avignon (Pont Saint-Bénézet): Famous for the children's song "Sur le Pont d'Avignon," this partially ruined bridge is rich in history and provides a stunning perspective of the Rhône River and surrounding surroundings.

Avignon's Old Town: Explore the tiny, cobbled alleyways dotted with charming shops, cafes, and historic structures, such as the majestic Avignon Cathedral and the bustling Place de l'Horloge.

Cultural Experiences

Avignon Festival: Held annually in July, this is one of the world's leading contemporary performing arts festivals. The city comes alive with official and fringe theater, dance, and music productions.

Local Markets: The Les Halles market in Avignon is an excellent way to learn about local culture and food, since it sells fresh produce, regional delicacies, and handmade crafts.

Practical Tips

Getting There: Avignon is easily accessible via train from Lyon and other major towns. The city can also be accessed by vehicle or bus.

Best Time to Visit: Spring and early autumn offer beautiful weather and fewer crowds, whereas summer is popular for the Avignon Festival.

Key Attractions in Arles include the well-preserved Roman Amphitheater (Arènes d'Arles), which holds concerts and bullfighting.

Alyscamps: An old Roman necropolis with a hauntingly beautiful avenue lined with sarcophagi that Van Gogh captured in his paintings.

Van Gogh's Legacy: Arles is closely connected with Vincent van Gogh, who painted some of his most famous works here. Visitors can follow the Van Gogh route to explore the locations that inspired his artwork.

Cultural Experiences

Photography and Art: The Fondation Vincent van Gogh and other local galleries exhibit modern and classic art, with a concentration on Van Gogh-inspired pieces.

Local festivals: The Arles Feria, a historic bullfighting festival, and the Rencontres d'Arles, a well-known photography festival, are major cultural events in the city.

Practical Tips

Getting There: Arles is easily accessible by train and car, making it an ideal day excursion from adjacent cities.

Best Time to Visit: The city is best visited in the spring and fall, when the weather is pleasant and cultural events are in full flow.

Other Notable Villages and Towns

Orange: Known for its historic Roman architecture, especially the Roman Theater and the Triumphal Arch, both UNESCO World Heritage sites. The town also has a long heritage of Roman culture.

Cultural Insights: The Chorégies d'Orange is an annual opera event hosted in the ancient theater that provides an unforgettable cultural experience.

Vaison-la-Romaine: This town has substantial Roman ruins, a large archeological site, and a well-preserved medieval upper town. It's an intriguing combination of ancient and medieval history.

Cultural Insights: The town offers a variety of cultural events and boasts a thriving arts scene, including theater and music festivals.

Gordes: A picturesque hilltop village with stone buildings and spectacular views of the Luberon Valley. Gordes is a typical Provençal village that is frequently seen in films and pictures.

Cultural Insights The village has long been a haven for artists, and it now organizes a summer music festival. The adjacent Abbaye de Sénanque is known for its lavender fields.

Practical Tips for Day Trips

Transportation and Access: These towns are easily accessible via public transportation, such as trains and buses. Car rentals are also a wonderful way to explore at your own pace.

Parking and Accessibility: Many old towns have narrow streets and restricted parking, so it's best to take public transportation or park outside the town center.

Dining and Accommodation: Each town has a range of dining alternatives, from local bistros to fine dining restaurants serving regional cuisine. For those looking to extend their stay, there are various options, including lovely bed and breakfasts and boutique hotels.

Activities and Itineraries: Suggested activities

include guided walking tours, local craft shops, vineyard visits, and natural park exploration. Day trip itineraries can be tailored to include a variety of cultural, historical, and outdoor activities.

Thank you so much for reading our travel guide to Rhone Valley! We hope it made your journey even more amazing. Got a minute, tell us what you think about the book. Your review can help fellow travelers and serve as an impetus for us to create better guides in the future. Safe Travel and happy adventure!

Made in the USA
Middletown, DE
31 August 2024

60134516R00106